PURE STYLE

PURE STYLE

JANE CUMBERBATCH

PHOTOGRAPHY BY

HENRY BOURNE

RYLAND
PETERS
& SMALL

Art Director **Jacqui Small**

Art Editor **Penny Stock**

Senior Editor **Sian Parkhouse**

Project Editor **Sophie Pearse**

Stylist **Jane Cumberbatch**

Assistant Stylist **Fiona Craig-McFeely**

Production **Vincent Smith**

DTP Manager **Caroline Wollen**

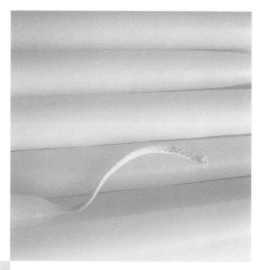

First published in Great Britain in hardcover in 1996
by Ryland Peters & Small, Cavendish House,
51–55 Mortimer Street, London W1N 7TD
Paperback edition first published in 2000
10 9 8 7 6

Text © Jane Cumberbatch 1996
Design and photographs
© Ryland Peters & Small 1996

Printed and bound in China by Toppan Printing Co.

Hardcover ISBN 1 900518 04 X
Paperback ISBN 0 84172 009 7

A CIP record for this book is available from
the British Library

Contents

INTRODUCTION

Pure Style is not just about rooms and furnishings, or about trying to achieve an impossibly perfect glossy lifestyle – *Pure Style* is about trying to achieve a balance. It's about making life luxurious, not in a costly, glitzy sense, but in a more matter-of-fact, practical and natural way. *Pure Style* is about paring down and trying to live with less clutter (the fewer things we have to fuss about, the more we can get on with living). It's about simple, basic design that combines function and beauty of form – crisp, clean, classic and timeless.

PURE STYLE IS

about being economical but without skimping on essential things like good food or a decent bed. *Pure Style* is not all about slavishly following fashions in interiors, it's about being practical and resourceful — tracking down great domestic staples that have been around forever, using the high street chain stores for good basic buys, or seeking out second-hand furniture that can be revitalized with a lick of paint. *Pure Style* focuses on the sensual side of living: such as texture — frothing soap, rough log baskets, string bags, a twiggy wreath entwined with fresh rosemary sprigs, or the bliss of sleeping in pure white cotton sheets; smell — fresh flowers, sweetly scented candles or laundry aired outside in

hot sun; tastes – good bread or new potatoes cooked with fresh mint; colour – light, bright, airy, matt shades inspired by nature, cow parsley, egg and calico whites, butter and straw yellows, bean greens, sea and sky blues, and earth tones; natural things – moss, lichen, shells, pebbles; scents – great coffee, chocolate and delicious wine; fabrics – good value, durable and decorative, in simple patterns like checks and stripes; basics– functional items that look good, such as a tin mug, a pudding basin or glass Kilner jars. *Pure Style* is about creating living, breathing spaces throughout the house. The book shows you how to be functional and practical in the kitchen, with durable work surfaces, proper cupboards and essential kitchen kit. *Pure Style* is about making the rituals of eating as sensual as is practicable or possible and shows you how simple ideas – white plates, starched linen and jars of cut flowers – can create pleasing and visually satisfying arrangements. *Pure Style* also demonstrates how plain but delicious basic ingredients – good cheese, fresh fish, fresh fruit and vegetables – are the key to hassle-free food preparation. In the sitting room, *Pure Style* illustrates how a combination of elements and textures, such as comfortable seating, beautiful fabrics in cotton, wool and muslin, and candlelight and blazing fires, help to make living rooms relaxing and peaceful. To help you slumber more soundly, *Pure Style* shows you the benefits of well-made beds and proper mattresses as well as the luscious qualities of crisp cotton bedlinen, snuggly warm woollen blankets and quilts. In the bathroom, the book demonstrates how access to plenty of piping hot water, together with soft cotton towels and wonderful scented soaps, can make bathing a truly sybaritic experience.

ELEMEN

T S

To touch, to hold, to look, to smell, to taste: the sensual aspects of life are there to be nurtured and encouraged. Engage the senses and explore the visceral elements around you. Douse your sensibilities with tactile elements; encourage and incorporate colour and texture into your home to make life an altogether more spirited and rewarding affair.

Colour

Use colour to make daily living more pleasurable, spirited and uplifting. Thinking about how colour appears in nature gives clues to choosing the sorts of colours you might want to have in your home. Neutrals are timeless and easy to live with, while white is unifying, restful and a favourite with those who seek a simple approach to living. Greens are versatile, ranging from the brightest lime to much sludgier tones, and earthy hues of brown can be used for a variety of looks. The sea and sky colours found in denim, on china, bedlinen and in paint give clarity and crispness to interior settings. Look at garden borders to appreciate the range of pinks and transfer these indoors as soft lilac walls or muted floral cottons. Creams and yellows. are cheerful, optimistic colours and have universal appeal. *Pure Style* is not about slavishly coordinated colour schemes, although it does show you how to put together rooms and interiors with accents on colour. It is more about considering the colours of everything around and incorporating them in our daily lives. Colour is a vital element in characterizing an interior and it need not be expensive. If you can't afford a complete redecoration, sub-tly change the emphasis with different cushions, covers and splashes of floral detail.

Whites

Milk

Egg white

Wax white

Bone

Oatmeal

Calico

Brilliant white, eggshell white, bone white, lime white, even plain old white, all come in a plethora of contrasting hues and tones. White creates a peaceful and timeless ambience which benefits both period, and starker contemporary settings equally. It is a minimalist's dream shade and makes for harmonious, unifying spaces. In today's super-charged, techno world it's good for the soul to retreat into a reviving white oasis where simplicity rules. For an all-white scheme, strip then paint floorboards in white floor paint and seal with a yacht varnish; use white emulsion on the walls and ceilings. So that the whole interior does not finish up looking too much like the inside of an icebox, create toning contrasts by giving the woodwork

touches of off-white, bone, or white with grey. For a unifying effect paint furniture in similar shades and add cotton drill slip-on covers, calico cushions and filmy muslin drapes. Complete with accessories such as white china and bedlinen, available from big department stores at bargain prices during the sales.

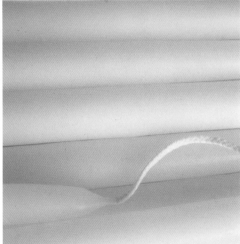

Blues

Blue spans a host of colour variations, from deep hyacinth to very pale ice. Blue can turn to lavender when mixed with violet, and turquoise when blended with green. In the middle of the spectrum are the purer blues of cornflower and bright powder blue. Take a cue from the fashion world and look at the soft blues that characterize denim as it is washed and worn. These shades adapt as easily to home furnishings as they do to jeans and jackets. Pale shades are the tones most likely to appear cold, especially in north-facing rooms. The trick here is to use warming devices, such as faded kelims or terracotta flower pots, perhaps in a room with duck-egg blue walls. If a pure blue is too strong for your taste then try a more sludgy mix of grey, green and blue – this works well with highlights of white; or try a dining room scheme in a sludge-blue, offset with white-painted furniture, curtains in blue-and-white check and bowls of white narcissi. For a more homespun look, combine the muted Shaker blues with red-and-white striped or checked cotton.

Washed blue

Sea

Beach-hut blue

Denim

Checked blue

Useful decorating details in blue include tartan china and clear glass. There is blue-and-white striped ticking for loose covers and storage bags. And for a jaunty beach-house theme, make chair covers in bright lavender-blue cricket stripe cotton, together with faded blue-jean cotton cushions (various denim weights are available from fabric wholesalers).

Leek

Spring green

Pea

Herb

Cabbage

Garden

Green

Green is one of the most accommodating colours for interiors. In a contemporary setting a vivid apple green or lime teamed with flourishes of fuchsia pink can work well, while traditional interiors call for duller shades mixed with grey, such as hopsack and olive. Take inspiration from the range of greens in nature; look at the bright lime-green stems of hyacinths or blades of fresh spring grass. Peas in their pods and cabbage leaves provide another source of vibrant and sometimes variegated greens. Try using sage-and-white striped cotton for chair covers with bursts of lime-green for cushions.

Pink and lavender

Pink needn't be the sickly colour we associate with frilly, little-girl bedrooms, over-the-top chintzy floral drawing rooms, or the monotonous peach-coloured bathrooms that are perennial in mass-produced home design catalogues. At the other extreme, shocking pink walls and ceilings are hardly a recipe for subtle, understated living. Careful selection and combining of pinks with other colours is therefore the key to making a stylish, comfortable statement. In contemporary settings fuchsia pink, lavender and green combine well – just look to the garden border for inspiration and think of purply lavender heads on sage-green foliage or foxglove bells with bright-green stalks and leaves. For a smart, up-to-the-minute scheme for a sitting room paint the walls white, cover chairs and sofas in pale lavender and make up cushions in plain fuchsia and lime-green cottons. Hot pink floral prints look great married with white walls and loose covers,

creating a fresh, crisp and simple look. More delicate pink schemes need careful consideration to avoid looking bland. For a pink, though not at all prissy bedroom, paint the walls a warm shade such as a pale rose with a hint of brown and furnish with an antique lavender-coloured patchwork quilt and calico Roman blinds – the whole effect will be clean and subtle.

Lilac

Marshmallow

Lavender

Foxglove

Hyacinth

On the edible front, think of enticing deep pink fresh strawberry ice cream; sticky and spongy marshmallows and violet cream chocolates. Less threatening to body shape are pink turnips, rhubarb, bitter radicchio leaves, and even pink pasta. For bright culinary detail try pink plastic textures, from mugs and brushes to buckets.

21

Earth and terracotta

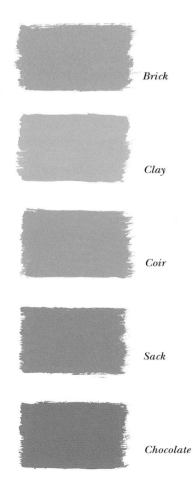

Brick

Clay

Coir

Sack

Chocolate

Because earthy hues are universally adaptable base colours it is hard to go wrong with them, except for those really drab mud-coloured schemes that were so popular during the seventies. Ranging from dark chocolate to cream, brown accents work in rustic and contemporary settings equally well. Consider the terracotta-

coloured façades prevalent through-out Provençe and Spain, the brown woodwork and detailing of an English cottage kitchen, or the terracotta flags and wood beams in a New England farmhouse. In contrast imagine a white, utilitarian urban loft with dark wood schoolhouse-style desks, tables, chairs and filing cabinets. Study the shades of soil,

from a clay-based red to a rich dark brown, and see how they act as a foil for brighter colours in nature. Clay pots are perfect for setting off the foliage and flowers of emerging spring bulbs. Be bold with earthy tones; for instance paint a dining room in a rich Etruscan shade for a warm effect both night and day.

Even boring beige is still a favourite shade and fabric companies love it for its versatility. Beige looks smart in various clever contemporary reworkings such as coir and natural fibre matting for floors, tough neutral linen for curtains and chair covers, or brown office files and filing boxes. Use striped and checked cotton in pinkish terracotta and white to make up chair covers and curtains with a wonderful natural feel.

Yellow

Creamy country yellows are wonderfully adaptable and open up the meanest and darkest rooms to increase a sense of space. When decorating, opt for the softer end of the yellow spectrum as acidic yellows are harder to live with because of their sharpness. However, don't go too pale, as at the other end of the scale very clear, light primrose shades can appear insipid. Creams and yellows look great with white, or even orange. Some shades look quite brown in the pot, but once on the walls are wonderfully rich and very well-suited to period hallways and kitchens. A slightly more acidic yellow will be lighter yet still rich in colour and should look good in artificial light and really glowing when the sun shines. There are also some very rich, bright yellows available and if you can stomach their intensity these gutsy shades illuminate and cheer up even the pokiest spaces, and look fabulous against blue-and-white china and furnishings. Cream or yellow looks good as paint on walls and as a decorative colour for furniture.

In a creamy kitchen, choose traditional stoneware pudding basins and white crockery to suit the simple theme. In living rooms, yellow walls look good against mustard-coloured check and plain cottons, with contrasting details in terracotta or blue. Yellows really come into their own in spring, when rooms are filled with daffodils and other spring flowers.

Butter

Honey

Pudding basin

Straw

Mustard

Texture

Scant attention is paid to our senses by the purveyors of today's technological gadgetry with their ever-increasing obsession for convenience and labour-saving devices. There is not much textural appeal, for example, about computer hardware, or mass-produced, static-inducing synthetic carpets and fabrics. In complete contrast, sensual textures like soft, wool blankets, crisp cotton bedlinen and light and downy pillows are the domestic staples handed down from past generations that help to bolster us against the more soulless elements of modern living. From the perfect smoothness of a baby's skin to the gnarled and ridged bark on a tree, natural textures are there for us to take notice of and appreciate. They often combine an alluring mix of qualities. For instance, lumps of volcanic pumice stone, logs and shells are defined as rough or smooth, depending on the degree of erosion upon them by wind, sun, fire and rain. It is this very naturalness that compels us to gather such things about the house.

Our homes need natural textures to transform them into living, breathing spaces — and polished wooden floors, rough log baskets, and pure cotton fabrics are just some of the organic ideas we can introduce to suggest this effect.

Smooth

Smooth things are often fresh, clean things and appear all round the house, especially in the kitchen and bathroom. Washing activities spring to mind, such as a handful of frothing soap, or a big plastic bucketful of hot soapy water. Satisfyingly smooth surfaces of crisp white tiling, marble or utilitarian stainless steel conjure up a sense of clinical, streamlined efficiency. In kitchens, culinary preparation is made more efficient and hygienic when work surfaces can simply be sluiced, wiped down and made pristine. Utensils such as sparkling stainless steel pots and pans also help to keep culinary operations running smoothly. I love to cook with a selection of worn wooden spoons which have somehow moulded to my grip after years of devoted use.

Smooth, cast-iron bath surfaces and ceramic tiled walls can be scoured and scrubbed, so helping to keep bathrooms squeaky clean. Indoors as well as out, natural surfaces such as slate or well-worn flags are texturally pleasing. Smooth elements exist in a diversity of guises, from crisp white tissue paper tied up with silk ribbon to polished floorboards. On a food theme, goodies include the wonderful slippery-smooth waxed paper that serious shops wrap cheese in, slender glass bottles of olive oil, or slivers of fine chocolate in layers of the thinnest silver paper. You can also bring naturally smooth objects, such as ancient weathered pebbles and scoured driftwood collected on an impromptu beach hunt, indoors for textural decoration,

Rough

One of my favourite possessions is a roughly hewn olive wood basket from Spain. Made from the winter prunings of olive trees it is silvery-grey in colour, robust in design and a sheer pleasure to touch and hold. The locals in Spain use such baskets to transport eggs and wild mushrooms, oranges or tomatoes from their vegetable patches – while mine in London is filled with kindling for the fire. Rough, tough and hairy flooring in sisal and coir is durable and even when woven into patterns it still looks like a simple texture. Equally, a rough terracotta tiled floor is not only satisfying to walk on but if it is not laid in exact uniformity it has the appearance of having been in place forever.

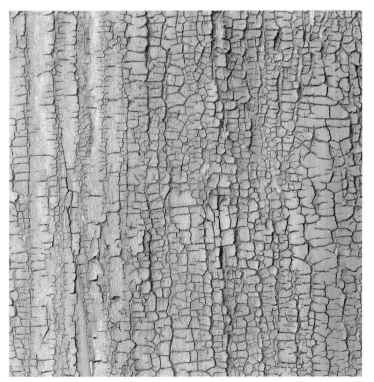

Rough textures in nature have usually been created by the elements, and even sun-blistered paint, a painter and decorator's nightmare, can create a visually pleasing finish on a weathered old outbuilding. This sense of roughness allied to age means that unevenly plastered or distemper-covered walls, or features such as reclaimed battered tongue-and-groove panelled doors, can make even a new house look rustic. Rough can mean contemporary too, and utilitarian concrete walls and floors are common features in industrial buildings converted to open, loft-style living spaces.

Roughness isn't always a pleasing texture, as anyone with chapped hands or prickly wool next to the skin knows, yet some fabrics such as cotton towels worn rough by repeated washing are perfect for an exhilarating rub down after a shower. And tools such as pumice stones and hard bristle brushes assist exfoliation and improve circulation.

Scent and taste

Scents and tastes are so evocative that childhood memories may be unexpectedly recollected with a certain waft of perfume or the aroma of a particular food. As a small girl on holiday in provincial hotels I invariably associated France with a cocktail of scents that included furniture polish, smelly plumbing and cooked garlic. In the same way, the first sweet grass cuttings of spring, evident as I pass by a newly mown field, park or suburban back garden, transport me back to games played on the lawn at my grandmother's house in Devon. Smells quicken our senses, increase anticipation and act as powerful stimuli – there is nothing like the whiff of strong coffee and toast to entice slothful risers out of bed. Taste is crucial to the pleasure we take in eating. Fresh ingredients are vital to making things taste good, together with a knowledge and appreciation of basic cooking skills. There is a world of difference between a home-made hamburger and the cardboard creations served up at fast-food outlets. Smell and taste are closely related, and one without the other would diminish the intensity of many edible experiences. Consider the first strawberry of summer; the heady flowery scent is a beguiling hint of the sweetness to come.

32

Flavour and fragrance

It is invigorating to have good smells around the house. I love paper-white narcissi whose flowers emit the most delicious sweet smell. Scented candles and bowls of pot pourri are other sources of floral scents. In the kitchen scents and tastes come to the fore: the fragrant citrus tang of grated lemon peel accompanies the preparation of sauces and puddings and the

earthy scent of wild mushrooms being fried rapidly in butter is any food lover's idea of heaven. Simple tastes are often the most sublime. What could be more enticing than a bowl of pasta mixed with garlic and a little olive oil, or a good, strong cheese? Herbs such as basil, rosemary, thyme and dill smell delicious and help to draw out the flavours of food.

Fabrics

Setting taste and aesthetic considerations aside, criteria for choosing one type of furnishing fabric over another include the suitability of the weight and weave for a type of furnishing and the fabric's ability to withstand the effects of wear and tear. Furnishing cotton, linen, wool, silk, synthetic and mixed fibres exist in a wealth of colours, textures and weights and with a little effort it should be possible to find just about anything you want at a price you can afford. If you fall for a really expensive fabric bigger than your budget, invest in a small amount for a cushion or two instead. Otherwise it's worth hunting in the sales for the larger quantities needed for upholstery. For good value basics go to an old-fashioned haberdashers and track down companies who supply television, film, theatre and artist's trades. These are great places to find varied weights of calico like those used for toiles in the fashion business, or extra wide widths of canvas used as stage backdrops, and cheap rolls of muslin that are employed by designers for costumes and sets. One popular silk specialist I know of carries stocks of coloured silks, including the type used for para-chutes. Over the next six pages you will find lots of examples of utility fabrics.

Light

Lighter weight fabrics are brilliant for simple, floaty window treatments. Make decorative half curtains from voile or muslin (see 24 and 27) panels with cased headings. Thread them onto narrow rods and anchor them within the window frame. Other lightweight curtain ideas include unlined cotton (see 6, 7, 8) or linen (see 22) drops with tapes or ribbon loops at the top. Basic roller blinds in fine fabrics (see 9) look subtle and understated in a cream or white decoration scheme. Spray stiffener might be useful to give body to some gauzy fabrics. Perfect for bedrooms and bathrooms are filmy transparent loose covers in voile (see 12) for chairs with pretty, curvy shapes. Soft Indian cotton in bright lime green (see 26) and other hot up-to-the-minute shades are great for making up colourful and inexpensive cushion covers. If you're in the mood, run up your own sheets, duvet covers and pillowcases in cotton sheeting (see 1), which comes in very wide widths. Covers should fit loosely around a duvet and have a generous opening secured with buttons, Velcro, or simple ties to make them easy to slip on and off. Printed cotton lawn dress fabric is also worth considering for sprigged floral pillow cases and cushion covers. Cotton sheeting is also a great staple for lightweight tablecloths and napkins. I keep a huge length in white for parties indoors and out, when we have to fit lots of people around mismatching tables.

For details of the fabrics shown on pages 38–43 see page 154

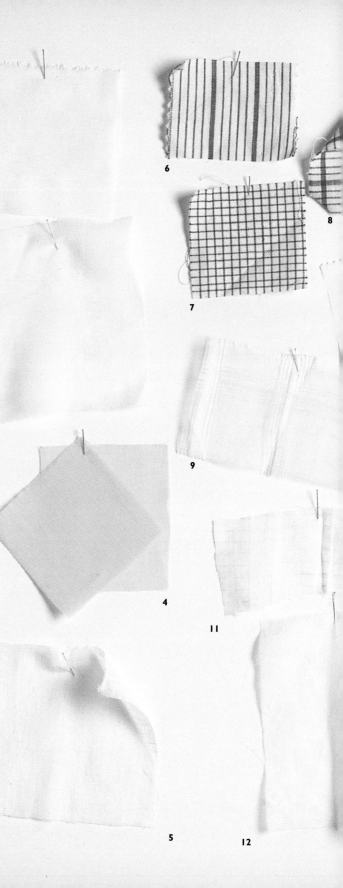

13

17

14

22

26

18

10

27

23

15

19

24

28

20

16

25

29

21

Versatile

I have a passion for blue checked cotton (see 34 and 60) and use it all around the house for crisp colour and detail; as cushions (see 58 and 59) for assorted chairs and as Roman blinds (see 34 and 59) in the dining and sitting room, Blue checked loose covers also look good, and can be as basic or as decorative as you want – with bows, piping, ties or button detailing, simple pleats, short skirts or flowing hemlines. Window seat cushions in cream linen with a piped trim are smart, and this fabric also works well as an idea for covers on daybed bolster cushions. If the fabric is not shrink resistant, and covers are to be washed rather than dry-cleaned, pre-wash all materials including piping before making up. Blue-and-white striped ticking, a robust cotton twill closely woven in narrow stripes and traditionally used for pillows and mattress covers, is also another favourite (see 45) and looks especially good as simple curtains with ties at my attic windows, and across an alcove that houses children's clothes. Ticking is also a smart, classic idea for chair and sofa covers. Continuing on a striped theme, an all-time favourite is a lightish weight lavender-blue-and-white printed cotton (see 47) that I've used for tablecloths and cricket chair covers for summer suppers out in the garden (see it made up as a flirty loose chair cover on pages 120–21). Another discovery is woven cotton roller towel, bought from a company that supplies towels to hospitals and other institutions. Supplied on a seemingly endless roll in convenient widths, it makes simple and useful chair covers (see pages 150–51).

30

31

36

37

38

32

33

39

34

35

40

47

54

60

62

48

55

61

49

63

42

50

57

64

51

56

65

44

58

66

45

52

53

59

67

Durable

Tough all-purpose fabrics include canvas (see 82 and 83), sometimes known as duck, that is great for garden chairs and awnings. It's also good for Roman blinds, bolster covers and as heavy duty laundry bags (see pages 138–39). Creamy coloured calico is one of the best fabrics ever invented – it's incredibly cheap but it manages to look smart and understated, and is durable, washable and perfectly practical. Calico comes in a number of weights; the finer qualities are more appropriate for loose covers or cushions, while thicker weights work well as insulating blinds (see 75), particularly if made in double thickness (see the Roman blind project on pages 100–101) or for making curtains. Tough cotton denim (see 69) looks good on chairs after it's been put through several very hot washes to fade its dark indigo colour. For a crisp, tailored look, or to show off techniques such as deep buttoning, chairs demand tight coverings to emphasize their shape. A self-patterned herby green cotton and viscose with simple tulips is one of my favourite upholstery fabrics (see it in yellow 87), and it looks great on one of my secondhand armchairs. Sofas with a contemporary feel look wonderful in solid sea green and blue colours in tightly woven cottons (see 88, 89, 90). Alternatively, plain cream cotton is stylish, but sensible for the dogless and childless only; choose some slightly more forgiving muddy-coloured linen if you have a family. Wool tartan (see 79) is another smart idea for upholstering the seats of dining chairs or sofas, and it also works well as throws for keeping warm on long cold winter's evenings.

68

69

70

74

75

71

72

76

73

77

78

82

83

87

93

84

88 89 90

94

80

85

91

95

81

86

92

96

Furniture

It may seem paradoxical, but I think that a diversity of objects can imbue an interior with a sense of character and uniformity. Old, new, decorative, industrial, contemporary or utilitarian, it's possible to combine a variety of furniture styles under one roof and yet create a strong visual statement. Fashion pundits and supermodels dictate the length of hemlines from season to season, but thankfully trends in interiors are less mercurial. But it is worth putting the same energies into assembling a look for your home as you would your wardrobe. As with desirable outfits, buy your furniture only after considering texture, comfort, shape and form. At home I have gathered together a hotchpotch of furniture from sales, second-hand shops and family — from 18th-century oak country dining chairs and old sofas to fold-up tables, painted junk sixties filing cabinets and kitchen chairs. My only proviso has been to weed out or revamp anything that I haven't liked the look of. Second-hand furniture

designed for industrial and commercial use, such as swivel architect's chairs, bookcases from libraries and pattern-cutting tables from factories, can be re-invented happily in a domestic setting, and is better quality than mass-produced equivalents.

Tables and chairs

A fold-up slatted beech chair, ideal for stowing away in small spaces, and an old wooden church chair – excellent durable seating for kitchens and dining rooms.

Stackable contemporary seating with beech-ply frame and splayed metal legs, inspired by the fifties butterfly chair by Arne Jacobsen.

Sturdy shapes in solid wood: a rustic beech chair with rush seating and a classic beech stool.

I like chairs that have no frills or gimmicky details, in other words, chairs that look good, are robustly constructed and comfortable to sit on. Classic country chairs with rush seats are ideal for kitchens and dining rooms. Fold-up wooden slatted seats, the staples of church halls the world over, can be stowed away and are excellent for use in small spaces.

A crisp bright pink cotton loose cover and a lick of white paint have given a junk chair a new lease of life.

A simple trestle table like this one in birchwood-ply has a multitude of uses, ranging from a work desk to an impromtu dining table.

You can see examples of this sixties-style weatherproof aluminium café chair in bars and cafés throughout Europe – a great idea for urban backyards and loft spaces.

Robust and utilitarian, a Swedish-style pine side table such as this could be used for displaying china, or books and flowers.

Big, basic and in solid pine: a definitive kitchen shape that would suit all kinds of interiors.

Essential folding shapes for indoors and out: a white slatted chair and a metal dining table.

A white lime paint effect is a resourceful device for sprucing up an old turn-of-the-century pine table like this one.

Customized with eggshell paint, this simple pine table would make a smart desk or sidetable anywhere in the house.

Like chairs, a table should look good, be strong and a pleasure to sit at. A basic table top perched on trestles is probably one of the most useful and portable shapes which can be set up or collapsed instantly. Junk shops are always good sources of chairs and tables alike — take your pick and revamp battered examples with a coat of paint.

Perfectly angled to support the sitter's back, this worn but elegant little factory chair is a good example of functional but stylish seating.

This crisp cotton checked cover with button detailing is a good idea for reinventing a basic calico-covered dining room chair.

Based on a fifties shape, a zinc-topped wooden table is a streamlined idea for a gleaming contemporary kitchen.

Beds

Beds should be chosen for both practical and visual considerations. To ensure many peaceful nights of slumber it is crucial at the outset of any bed-buying exercise to invest in a decent mattress, and a solid base or frame. If you have limited funds think about ways of revamping your existing bed. For instance, lovely bed linen and blankets can disguise even the ugliest of divan shapes.

right *A traditional cast iron bed frame suits all kinds of interiors.*

below right *A Shaker-inspired pine four-poster (an amazingly good value flat-pack) is painted in white eggshell for a smart understated finish.*

below *Spare in shape and detail, and perfectly functional, this superbly streamlined bed in Douglas fir is a minimalist's dream.*

Sofas and seating

Good springs and sound construction are essential for comfortable upholstered seating. It's worth buying a good second-hand sofa or armchair with a wooden frame and strong interior springs, stuffing and webbing, rather than something new and less sturdily put together. Cover sofas in tough upholstery weights of linen and wool, or devise loose covers which can be as basic as a throwover sheet, or opt for a tailored pull-on design in washable cotton.

top left *A Victorian chesterfield sports decorative button detailing.*
left *This romantic French daybed is good for tight spaces.*
above *A contemporary shape, excellent for sprawling out on.*
right *A Swedish-style wooden sofa with check covers, and a generously proportioned armchair.*

Cupboards and storage

In an ideal world storage should be devised to leave maximum living and breathing space. In reality we are hampered by budget, cramped rooms, too little time, too many occupants and too much clutter to set about the task of arranging ourselves a little more efficiently. Here are some ideas to make clearing away a more fruitful and inspiring exercise. Basic wooden shelving is one of the cheapest means of stowing everything from kitchen paraphernalia to bathroom towels, or scores of books. Free-standing storage notions include simple flat-pack systems — these are basic structures in pine that are good for utility rooms and children's rooms. If home is an attic flat with poor access, put together flat-pack cupboards or wardrobes on site.

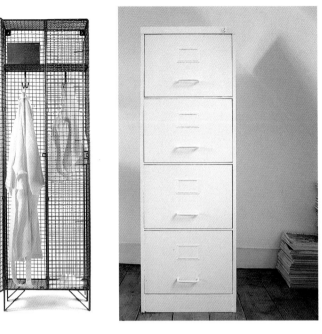

top left *Remember school cloakrooms? This metal mesh wardrobe is great for small spaces.*

top and far right *Bought cheaply from second-hand shops, this filing cabinet and simple chest of drawers were improved by a coat of paint.*

right *Inexpensive but stylish flat-pack cardboard drawers, designed for papers and home office work, but also ideal for storing odds and ends.*

far left *Laminated drawers with wire baskets are a clever reincarnation for flat-pack kitchen units.*
left *In natural wood, a classic pine cupboard is a smart kitchen staple.*
below left *A walk-in wardrobe is one of the most effective ways of stowing away everything from clothes to suitcases.*
below *A decorative wooden dresser or* visellier *like this looks at home in country settings.*

Objects

If we all made inventories of our possessions how many things could we designate as being not really useful, or something we hate but can't give away because it was a present or a family heirloom? It might be painful for your conscience, but in the long run paring down unnecessary household clutter eases the path to a more practical and soothing existence. Don't be sentimental about hoarding items that you'll never use. Identify the things that give you pleasure to hold, to use and look at. It's more useful to have one really good saucepan rather than have three second-rate ones that burn everything you cook. Even something as basic and utilitarian as a slender wood and bristle broom is a thing of beauty and just as humbly aesthetic as the rough mesh structure of a metal sieve, or a good old-fashioned mixing bowl whose deep curvy proportions are perfectly evolved to perform its tasks. Do away with those dusty lampshade bases made from Chianti wine bottles that your mother gave you for your first flat. But resurrect classic anglepoise desk lights, as those in the know continue to appreciate their supple proportions. Vernacular objects so perfectly designed to fulfil their function are works of art in their own right.

Utensils

Wooden chopping boards are kitchen staples: from slicing vegetables to serving up bread, and beech trivets protect kitchen surfaces from hot pans.

String is indispensable, from sealing jam pots to making an emergency washing line. And keep a supply of wooden spoons, for all mixing, stirring and beating operations. To extract spaghetti from a pan use a spoon with teeth.

A capacious flip-top stainless steel bin will take large amounts of kitchen rubbish, while a wood and bristle broom, found in any hardware store, is an essential tool for clearing up.

Whenever I have to make do with a temporary or makeshift kitchen during house renovations the surrounding chaos is bearable so long as I've had access to water, something to cook on (even if it's just a two-ringed portable stove) and a fridge. My survival kit of kitchen tools under such siege conditions includes a cast-iron enamelled cooking pot in which

A glass citrus fruit squeezer is a nifty tool for producing small amounts of orange, lemon, lime or grapefruit juice.

Found in just about every continental kitchen, a classic stove-top espresso maker is an easy way to make steaming-hot strong coffee.

Life would be impossible without a really good sharp stainless steel knife, a pair of scissors and a corkscrew!

Produce mounds of crisp, crunchy vegetables that really keep their flavour, or poach small pieces of fish, with a heavy-bottomed stainless steel steamer.

A robust cast-iron enamelled casserole is excellent, whether you are cooking for a crowd of friends, a simple family meal or just for one or two.

Drain everything from pasta and rice to salad leaves with a simple metal colander, and borrow or buy a fish kettle to take the angst out of cooking large fish like salmon in one piece.

For fishy treats: a strong oyster knife with a protective guard, and classic cutlery with bone-handled knives.

to conjure up everything from early-morning breakfast porridge to herby chicken casseroles, a sharp knife, a solid chopping board, a pile of wooden spoons, and, to keep spirits from flagging and the caffeine levels high, a metal stove-top espresso maker. Other crucial equipment includes scissors, a garlic crusher and, of course, a decent corkscrew.

Some of my favourite tools: a garlic crusher (that also stones olives), a balloon whisk and fish crackers, ideal for attacking crab.

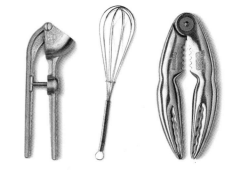

Some basic metal tools: a sieve for sifting flour or draining vegetables and a boxy grater for demolishing hunks of cheese such as Parmesan.

What kitchen would be complete without a kettle? Invest in a sturdy and hard-wearing metal catering one for endless rounds of satisfying brew-ups.

Wonderful to hold, and perfectly proportioned, a stainless steel frying pan for rustling up everything from risotto to fishsteaks.

Lighting

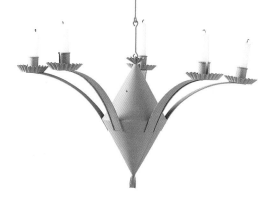

We can appreciate that daylight is the perfect light, because there is the dark with which to compare it. But night suffuses everything with its own particular mood and bestows its own impressions and textures. Without darkness we would be deprived of the luxury of candlelight which is the most sensual, calming and benign of all sources of light. Lit candles highlight a dark room with luminous flickering qualities that bring us in touch with the sensations of a pre-electric age. For a really romantic dining room, invest in a simple metal or wooden chandelier and light it with candles at every opportunity. At its best, artificial lighting is subtle and effective. At its worst, the glaring horrors of naked light bulbs or the bland brightness of supermarkets and airport lounges speak for themselves. The most sensitive way to light interiors is with pools of subtle illumination, achieved with lamps set in designated corners, or with recessed low-voltage downlighters.

Different ideas for candle holders range from simple painted wood or metal chandeliers to pleated flameproof shades with brass suppports – as the candle burns the shade moves with it. For summer evenings, choose from curvy glass hurricane shades, lanterns and nightlights (easily found in hardware stores).

Utilitarian lamps and
worklights look great in
contemporary and more
traditional settings alike.
Overhead pendant lights
in spun aluminium work
well in kitchen and dining
rooms, or as stylish hall
lighting. For desk tops,
thirties-style anglepoise
lights are not only smart
but flexible practical
gadgets that help illumi-
nate all kinds of tasks.

Storage

Many small-scale storage ideas can be customized to look individual and imaginative. Reinvent old shoe boxes, for example, by covering them with fabric or paint to make colourful storage for your home office or for children's toys. Or use a lick of white paint to transform an ugly black clothes rail into a stylish moveable wardrobe, ideal for small living spaces; it can be covered with a white sheet to keep the dust off. I am an avid collector of old jam jars, and other domestic basics that double up as stylish containers include metal buckets (good for vegetables) and glass Kilner jars (they make even staples like rice, flour and pasta look good). Industrial meat hooks are available from good kitchen shops and are a great way to hang up your *batterie de cuisine*.

A wooden vegetable crate, procured free from the local greengrocer, is smartened up with lime emulsion.

A junk shop basket is a useful solution for bulky items such as this thick checked blanket made in Wales and cushions covered in blue and green cotton.

Empty jam jars with neat, good-looking proportions are ideal for accommodating anything from pens and pencils to flowers.

A simple pine chest of drawers has all manner of uses, from organizing an untidy desk top, to housing fabric samples in a studio.

Empty wall space can be put to good use with a simple Shaker-style peg rack. These bags are made from washable cotton.

Paint a stack of boxes in a single colour like these Shaker-style ones, coated in bright blue emulsion.

Glass jars are utilitarian and smart and can be filled with flour, sugar or pasta, or used for their original purpose, preserving.

A painted flat-pack cabinet is decorative and practical, for display and storage.

Hang meat hooks from poles for instant hanging space. This old broom handle is supported by metal fittings.

Recycle old shoe boxes and cover them with bright cotton fabric as an attractive storage solution in the office, or for children's toys.

An ugly black clothes rail has been transformed by a lick of white paint into a stylish and moveable wardrobe, ideal for small living spaces. It can be covered with a white sheet to keep the dust off.

For a smart contemporary look stash spoons and cutlery in metal pots and arrange them in rows on shelves and kitchen surfaces, where they are handy for use.

A wooden two-tiered shoe rack, reminiscent of school cloakrooms, is useful for hallways and bedrooms.

Display

above *Cheap wooden frames painted in varying earthy shades of emulsion, mounted with old postcards of beach scenes, look great arranged in serried rows on plain white walls.*
right *A favourite collection of old pudding basins is arranged simply in an old corner cupboard.*

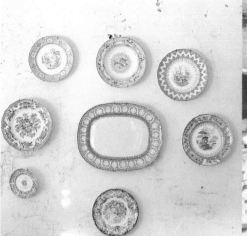

Making a statement about the way you display favourite things, from photographs to kitchen pots and pans, is all part of creating order and giving your living space a characteristic look. There is something arresting to the eye to see collections of basic vernacular objects – even something as common or garden as plain white mugs can look good en masse.

Use natural elements to devise beautifully simple display ideas such as collections of pebbles from the beach; shadow boxes filled with leaves, shells and china fragments from the shoreline; bowls or jars planted with your favourite spring bulbs; and collections of roughly hewn olive baskets.

China and glass

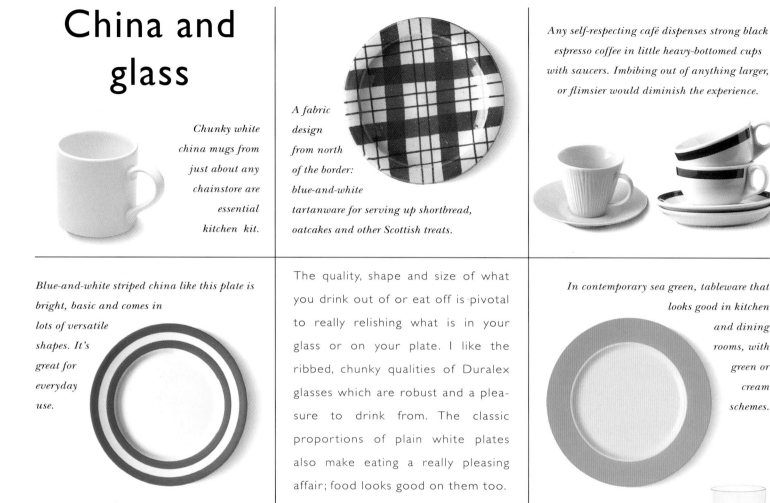

Chunky white china mugs from just about any chainstore are essential kitchen kit.

A fabric design from north of the border: blue-and-white tartanware for serving up shortbread, oatcakes and other Scottish treats.

Any self-respecting café dispenses strong black espresso coffee in little heavy-bottomed cups with saucers. Imbibing out of anything larger, or flimsier would diminish the experience.

Blue-and-white striped china like this plate is bright, basic and comes in lots of versatile shapes. It's great for everyday use.

The quality, shape and size of what you drink out of or eat off is pivotal to really relishing what is in your glass or on your plate. I like the ribbed, chunky qualities of Duralex glasses which are robust and a pleasure to drink from. The classic proportions of plain white plates also make eating a really pleasing affair; food looks good on them too.

In contemporary sea green, tableware that looks good in kitchen and dining rooms, with green or cream schemes.

Tables decorated on a clean white theme look good with injections of bright colour like this vibrant yellow glass.

Workaday glassware for knocking back iced water, slugs of sherry, bubbly and other thirst quenchers.

A choice of vessels for dedicated coffee drinkers: tiny chocolate brown cups for small shots of pure caffeine, like espresso, or a heavy-bottomed cup for capuccino.

Jolly blue-and-white checked china is a cheery sight on the breakfast table. This shallow bowl is useful for dishing up cornflakes and other morning staples.

A classic jug shape that has been around for ever – they come in lots of different sizes and they also make great vases for flowers.

Classic white bone china plates are my favourites, and make the humblest meal look really appetizing.

Blue-and-white spongeware: very decorative for informal settings, and it also looks good on dressers and shelves.

You can't beat plain blue-and-white bone china for simple and stylish kitchen schemes – one of my all-time favourites.

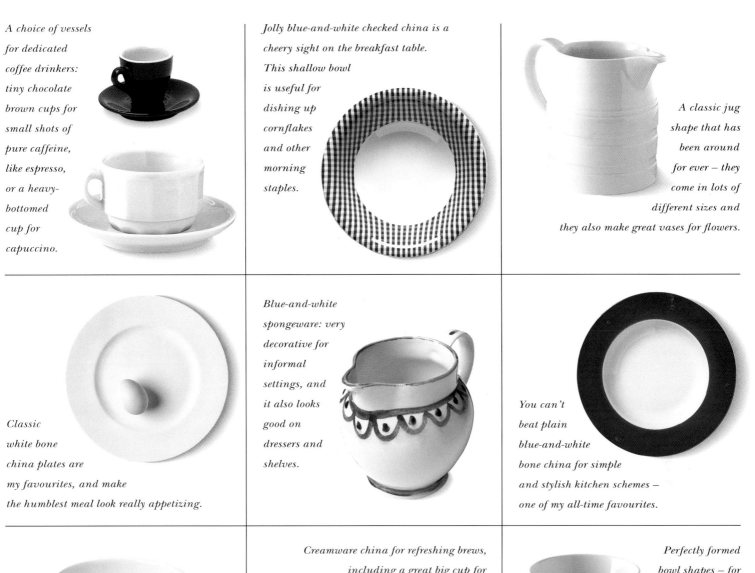

Creamware looks brilliant in country cream painted kitchens, or dining rooms with decorating details in white and other neutrals.

Creamware china for refreshing brews, including a great big cup for warming milky breakfast coffees.

Perfectly formed bowl shapes – for serving everything from porridge and puddings to soups and salads.

PUTTING IT ALL
TOGETH

ER

Colour and comfort are key ingredients in putting rooms together. Bright, light, airy shades of white and cream create inviting spaces, as do stronger greens, lavenders and blues. Choose furniture that combines function with style, and stick to basic shapes. Think about texture to help bring life into your surroundings; draw from nature for inspiration.

Culinary living

There are an awesome number of items that need to be squeezed into the average kitchen: boxes of breakfast cereals, pots, pans, dishwasher, fridge, sink – the list is endless. Storing and incorporating it all requires planning and thought. Cupboards, drawers, shelves and work surfaces should be considered both for functional and aesthetic appeal. Make surfaces durable and use basic materials like wood, marble, slate and stainless steel. Pare down your kitchen kit to the most basic essentials. Make the daily rituals of eating as pleasurable as is possible or practical. Eat off simple white plates, drink from good glasses, light candles, fill jars with flowers and spread a crisp white linen cloth for special occasions. Preparing food can be a therapeutic experience even if you are busy with work or family. Avoid food fashions (what is it this month – French, Italian or outer Mongolian?) and resist long-drawn-out recipes with impossible-to-find ingredients. Don't become a nervous wreck looking for exactly the right type of extra-virgin olive oil. Stick to food that you like and do well. It's far better to serve up an excellent cheese on toast than a second-rate and unremarkable attempt at something more flashy.

right *Wooden kitchen cupboards and drawers constructed from basic carcasses and painted in tough, matt creamy eggshell textures create understated and smart storage for kitchen kit.*

In the past, kitchens were purely rooms in which to prepare and cook food, while dining rooms were set apart as separate rooms dedicated to eating. To meet the demands of late 20th-century living, kitchens have evolved as spaces which fulfil all sorts of functions, so that eating and living are frequently combined. Different settings dictate different priorities. Rural kitchens need to cope with the toing and froing of muddy feet or paws and are the natural habitats of wonderful warming stoves such as Agas and Rayburns, which are both practical and stylish machines.

In town, there is more emphasis on the clever siting of labour-saving devices such as dishwashers, electric juicers, microwaves and so on, to help deal with the pressures of city life.

Most food preparation takes place on durable surfaces and there are various options. Oiled regularly and kept pristine with frequent scrubbing, worktops in maple or beech are the ultimate luxury, albeit a costly one. A cheaper solution is to buy lengths of beech block from large DIY outlets. Salvage yards are also a good source of reclaimed timber for work surfaces, for example I found a bargain teak draining board from a Victorian

almshouse at a country salvage yard. Despite its association with glossy Hollywood-style bathrooms, marble is a robust, hygienic material and unpolished matt grey, white or creamy textures make practical, understated work surfaces. Marble is particularly affordable at source, for instance in southern France, Spain and Italy. For a really cheap kitchen facelift, laminated plywood is available in lengths from builders' merchants and comes in lots of different colours. The sink is a crucial part of the kitchen work surface and chunky, deep white ceramic Belfast sinks are ideal and can be picked up quite easily second-hand.

left *Clean uncluttered kitchens, with pots and pans neatly stowed away in cupboards or on shelves, are comfortable places where you can lay a big table and entertain your friends in style.*

Painted storage

Create stylish storage on a budget with utilitarian basics such as painted tin cans, green grocer's vegetable crates and terracotta flower pots.

TINS MATERIALS

tins

eggshell paint

2.5 cm (1 in) paint brush

CRATES MATERIALS

vegetable crates

eggshell paint

2.5 cm (1 in) paint brush

FLOWER POTS MATERIALS

terracotta flower pots

matt emulsion paint

2.5 cm (1 in) paint brush

fine paint brush to apply design

pencil

small glass jars

TINS

Recycle used tin cans – baked beans and tomato cans are ideal – and paint them to create smart storage for kitchen utensils.

INSTRUCTIONS

1. Remove the lids with the type of tin opener that takes off the entire lid, leaving a clean edge on the can and no lip.

2. Wash the empty cans in hot soapy water to remove the labels. If any glue remains, gently sand with a fine sandpaper. Sand the top rim to take off the sharp edge.

3. Apply two coats of eggshell paint, inside and out.

CRATES

Beg wooden vegetable crates from a friendly green-grocer and jazz them up with paint to make jolly kitchen storage. Paint them in various shades of country-kitchen creams or be inventive and experiment with bright blues, greens and yellows, as shown here. As an alternative to vegetable crates, you can attack any kind of box with a paint brush – oyster cartons, shoe boxes and even cereal packets can all be used to make colourful, almost instant storage.

INSTRUCTIONS

1. Wipe down the vegetable crates with a damp cloth and sand lightly to remove any splintered wood. Pull out any nails which are sticking out. and remove labels by scrubbing them with hot water or sanding them away.

2. Once the crates are prepared and dry, apply two coats of paint, sanding between coats.

FLOWER POTS

Introduce splashes of colour to a room with flower pots decorated in pinks, lavenders or any other strong shade. Experiment with motifs – checks, stripes and scallops are just three to consider.

INSTRUCTIONS

1. Before you begin, wash the flower pots, giving them a good scrub with a hard brush to remove all traces of soil and dirt.

2. Leave them to dry out thoroughly in a warm place; any moisture left in the clay will stain the painted finish.

3. Apply two coats of white emulsion paint. When the paint is dry take a pencil and lightly draw your design directly onto the pots.

4. Paint over the pencil lines in a contrasting colour using a fine brush. Take care not to overload it with paint as you will have less control of your brush strokes. It is a good idea to blot the brush on some scrap paper first to remove excess paint and to steady your hand. If any pencil lines still show when you have finished, remove them with a clean, soft eraser after the paint has dried.

5. Place flowers in a glass jar of water and put in the pot. The painted pots are not weatherproof and should not be left outside in rain.

left *Open wooden shelving left in bare wood or painted in the same colour as the rest of the kitchen is a practical and decorative way to display china, kitchen tins and containers.*

Storage solutions are key to creating a well-organized kitchen. At the most basic level simple, open shelves in pine are incredibly useful vehicles for housing plates, glasses, culinary herbs and just about any other kitchen paraphernalia. Collections of tins and boxes in interesting shapes and colours make an attractive display. Screw cup hooks to the underside of pine shelving and you have instant hanging space for mugs, ladles, sieves and whisks. Not everyone is keen to have their kitchen contents on view, so cupboard doors hung on a basic carcass are the perfect camouflage for larder contents or a repertoire of pots and pans.

Wall-to-wall units and cupboards are practical but some custom-made schemes with fancy trims and detailing can be fantastically expensive. For a more individual look – and if you are strapped for cash anyway – combine a minimum of built-in elements such as a sink, cooker and worktop in a unit, together with free-standing features such as a second-hand dresser base jazzed up with paint, or an old metal factory trolley which is ideal for wheeling plates and dishes around. Other useful storage notions include a wall-mounted wooden plate drainer, or a tall, free-standing larder cupboard, ideal for filing with heavy items like tins, groceries and china.

right *A bright, cheerful kitchen with a utilitarian feel. Pride of place is given to a magnificent forties cooker that deals with cooking operations as efficiently as any contemporary model. Crisp blue-and-white checked lino floor tiles and a cotton tablecloth complete the homey, relaxed atmosphere.*

top left *Practical and functional: a wonderfully deep granite double sink that allows different washing operations to be carried out at the same time, a great idea for large families, or busy cooks who create a lot of washing up.*

centre left *Wooden shelving studded with cup hooks is a space-saving way of storing rows of smart blue-and-white mugs and basic drinking glasses.*

left *Although kitchen drawers are not an imme-diately obvious solution for storing china, in the absence of cupboards they work extremely well.*

right *In the streamlined and minimalist reinven-tion of a London terraced house, the area beneath the staircase has been art-fully designed to contain storage behind a series of white lacquered flush-fitting cupboard doors.*

CULINARY LIVING

*Kitchen elements with a
smooth, streamlined and
contemporary edge are
definitely no-go areas for
clutter and chaos. Materials
such as marble and zinc are
practical worktop ideas,
whilst pans in durable
stainless steel look great.*

left *Blue-and-white striped cotton roller towel, used for chair covers or for table runners as here, can be sourced from specialist companies who supply institutions (see the project on pages 150–51 to make your own chair covers).*

below *Crisp plain white cotton tablecloths work in any setting. A row of narcissi planted in big pudding bowls creates simple, colourful and scented decoration for parties and everyday use.*

Eating and drinking, however humble and low-key an affair, should be revelled in and made the most of. As well as deciding what to eat at any particular meal, what to eat it off and what sort of mood you want to convey are of equal importance. At the end of a gruelling day with three children there are few frills at my table, but it's still worth lighting candles or finding some ironed linen napkins to create a sense of occasion. Table settings needn't be elaborate affairs. Pleasing textures and well-made glass, china and cutlery are the crucial elements. On a day-to-day basis you might settle for a crisp check cloth with a jar of garden flowers, basic white plates and simple glass tumblers. When friends come it's worth pushing the boat out and laying a crisp, white linen cloth and napkins, together with candles, your best bone-handled cutlery and wine glasses.

The sales are brilliant sources of discounted china and where I go to buy seconds of white Wedgwood bone china plates. Street markets and junk shops are useful for single pieces of antique glass. During a weekly hunt around my local market in London's East End, I pounced upon half a dozen late-Victorian heavy wine glasses, each one different, and use them to serve up everything from jellies to drinks. Department stores are good for table linen, together with an ever-growing number of mail-order companies. Alternatively, you could make your own tablecloths and napkins from specially wide linen from fabric wholesalers, or run up fabric by the yard or metre. If you're really stuck, simply use a plain white sheet. And if you have a children's party to organize, buy plain white disposable paper cloths available from most chainstores.

One of the best things about assembling table settings is thinking of natural greenery and floral components for decoration. In the autumn, plates of nuts or leaves look striking and so do vases of branches studded with bright red berries. At Christmas time I spray apples with gold paint and put them in a big wooden bowl for decoration on the table, or hang them on string from a chandelier. I also scatter small branches of Christmas tree cuttings on the table and for some early seasonal colour and scent there are pots

Wooden dining chairs come in a variety of shapes. Don't worry if yours aren't all the same design: a mix of styles, sourced from second-hand and junk shops, can look just as good as a fully matching set.

above *Plain white china plates, bowls and cups look great against any colour scheme, and always make food look appealing, however humble your offering. Specialist catering shops can often yield good buys.*

of flowering narcissi or hyacinths. In early spring I like to fill metal buckets with the bright green sticky buds of chestnut branches or pussy willow, but summer tables are the most fun to create: I pick nasturtiums and sweet peas from my back yard and bring home armfuls of cow parsley after a day out in the countryside. Even a few jugs of fresh herbs, like rosemary, thyme, lavender or parsley make basic but beautiful decorations. Sometimes we've rented a cottage in Cornwall and there the summer hedgerows are thick with leggy purple foxgloves which are stunning for table embellishments simply stuffed into tall, clear glass jars and vases.

On trips to Spain everyone eats outside in the evening sitting around trestle tables laid with grilled fish, meat, pasta, bread, wine and cheese. After the glut of wild spring blooms such as orchids, daisies, buttercups, campion and lilies, it's harder to find flowers during the months of summer drought. A useful source is the local village market where squat, dark-skinned ladies sell white tuberoses, a few stems of which produce a glorious intoxicating scent as night falls. Otherwise the table is decorated with vases of silvery-grey olive cuttings. We get the barbecue going and cook up everything from sardines to slivers of pepper, courgette and aubergine.

left *Soft lilac emulsion on the walls is a good foil for covers in calico and a plain white cloth. A lime green checked cotton curtain and single stems of purple anemones provide a colourful contrast in this fresh and inviting dining set-up for two.*

Making preserves

These recipes, savoury and sweet, have one thing in common: they are simple and satisfying to prepare, use fresh, natural ingredients, and are absolutely delicious. Choose from an aromatic pesto sauce for pasta, rich strawberry jam and deliciously sweet and smooth lemon curd.

STRAWBERRY JAM INGREDIENTS

1 kg (2 lb) strawberries, washed and patted dry, then hulled
1 kg (2 lb) sugar with pectin
juice of a lemon

PESTO INGREDIENTS

50 g (2 oz) basil leaves
50 g (2 oz) pine nuts
3 garlic cloves
175 ml (6 fl oz) olive oil
50 g (2 oz) grated Parmesan and
50 g (2 oz) grated pecorino (or double the amount of Parmesan)

LEMON CURD INGREDIENTS

grated rind and juice of 4 lemons
4 very fresh eggs
125 g (4 oz) butter, cut into small pieces
375 g (12 oz) caster sugar

STRAWBERRY JAM

Wonderful simply spread on toast with butter, strawberry jam can be stirred into fromage frais for a simple pudding; layered between sponge, cakes,

dolloped on scones with cream, or used as a base for tarts and pies.

METHOD

1. Place all the ingredients in a large preserving pan. Heat gently until the sugar is thoroughly dissolved, and the strawberries have softened and broken down, but have not completely lost their shape. Stir frequently.

2. Bring to the boil and boil steadily for about four minutes or until setting point is reached To test for this spoon a little jam onto a cold plate and allow it to cool. If setting point is reached it should hold its shape when it is pushed gently with a finger. If this does not happen continue to cook and test again at frequent intervals.

3. Remove from the heat and skim off any scum with a metal slotted spoon. Leave to stand for 15–20 minutes to prevent the fruit rising in the jars.

4. Stir the jam gently then pot and cover with wax discs, wax side down, and cellophane rounds.

PESTO

Marked by the delicious herby and aromatic qualities of basil, this simple Italian sauce can be put together in a matter of minutes, and all of the ingredients are readily available from good delicatessans and supermarkets. It is fabulous with pasta; stir in two tablespoons for every serving and top with more grated Parmesan. Use it to accompany grilled fish or as a filling for baked potatoes.

METHOD

Place all the ingredients, except the cheeses, in a blender and whizz to a rough paste. Then stir in the cheese. Serve immediately or store in covered jars in the refrigerator and use within three days.

LEMON CURD

Making curd is one of the most delicious ways of preserving fruit. Limes and oranges both make very good curd but the traditional favourite is lemon curd. Do not make huge quantities in any one batch as the mixture will heat through unevenly and be likely to curdle. Lemon curd is delicious by the spoonful straight from the pot. Less gluttonous suggestions include spreading it on bread, using it as pancake filling or for lining the bases of fruit flans and pies, or making traditional individual lemon curd tartlets. Or try serving it as a delectable pudding in tiny pots with homemade shortbread.

METHOD

1. Place all the ingredients in the top of a double saucepan or in a deep heatproof bowl standing over a pan of simmering water. Do not allow the base of the bowl to touch the boiling water.

2. Stir until the sugar has dissolved and continue heating gently, without boiling, for about 20 minutes or until the curd is thick enough to coat the back of a wooden spoon.

3. Strain the curd into jars and cover with wax discs, wax side down, and cellophane rounds. Serve immediately or store in the refrigerator and use within three days.

   Substitute the lemons with limes or oranges for other fruit curds.

Table embellishments can be simple yet striking:
left *Topiary shapes work well in terracotta flower pots. Try a leggy myrtle standard, like the one shown here, or other shapes in box or bay.*
above *A pretty candelabra, a lucky find in a Roman market, looks especially lovely at night.*

The seating arrangements of any dining area are dependent upon the space that's available. If it is limited, tables and chairs might need to be of the fold-up variety and stowed away when necessary. On the other hand, generously proportioned rooms can accommodate big wooden refectory tables, or oval and round shapes and deep comfortable seating. Don't worry about having sets of matching chairs as disparate shapes, especially junk wooden kitchen chairs, can look quite good together and if you want to create a sense of unity you can cover them in simple pull-on loose covers in calico, or some other durable and washable texture. (See pages 78-79 for some colourful examples in blue-and-white striped roller-towel cotton, and the project on pages 150-51 for instructions on how to make your own.)

Choose a table to suit the style of the rest of the dining area. Rustic farmhouse shapes in wood look good almost anywhere and are practical and robust. Very contemporary streamlined models with zinc, stainless steel or laminated surfaces suit more modern settings. If furniture classics are your penchant, look to early 20th-century designs, such as simple ladderback oak chairs and solid oak tables, or more recent classics such as the sensually moulded white bucket-shaped Tulip chairs from the 1950s, shown on page 87. Since most people prefer suites of brand new dining furniture, excursions to markets and probing among second-hand shops can yield fantastic buys at bargain prices. If you need to make extra table space for a party you can make a very basic dining table from a piece of board or even an old door laid over a pair of trestles; simply disguise the makeshift base in a plain white sheet.

Other useful elements for dining areas include a side table or sideboard from which

left and above *Refectory style: a plain table and benches in solid Douglas fir pine are spare and minimal solutions for dining. Equally streamlined are the full-length limestone bench seating down one wall and the open fireplace.*

right *Low-backed wooden office chairs on wheels and a mahogany door laid on metal trestles are inventive ideas that are well suited to the wide-open contemporary living space in this converted London industrial building.*

to serve food or to display flowers or lighting. It's always handy to have supplies of plates, bowls and glasses close at hand, either stored on open shelving or in cupboards.

One of the highlights of winter is to be able to enjoy an open fire. If you are lucky enough to possess a working fireplace, gather some logs and kindling (or be practical and have them delivered) and give your guests the luxury of a warming blaze. Candlelight is the best and most romantic light to eat by. I buy creamy coloured church candles from a candlemaker at a nearby Greek Orthodox Church. If you don't possess particularly nice candlesticks, stick the candles on plain white plates or leave them free-standing for subtle illumination.

right *More colourful treatments for dining rooms include the yellow, green and blue scheme shown here. Pale cream walls in eggshell create a plain backdrop for splashes of more vibrant colours such as blue-and-white checked cotton Roman blinds, sofa cushions in lime green and blue, and a simple metal chandelier in matt yellow emulsion. On the table, the plastic green checked cloth, available by the metre from department stores, is smart and practical for everyday use. Flowering spring bulbs, bought cheaply by the tray from a local market, and planted in painted flower pots, provide scent and sunny detail.*

Relaxed living

Even the most frenetic workaholics need time to sink into a comfortable chair, put their feet up and contemplate life. It's good to be nurtured by music, soft cushions or a blazing fire. Living rooms are tailored to meet the demands of their occupants – families with small children require battle-proof chairs and fabrics, while single individuals with no danger of sabotage by sticky hands might make a sumptuous wall-to-wall white scheme their priority. But whatever your family status, gender or age, comfort and texture are the most important factors for rooms in which you want to wind down. Use colours that soothe and are light enhancing – such as soft creams or bone whites – and keep paint textures matt. Buy really solid comfortable upholstery, and proper feather-filled cushions. Be selective with the fabric textures that you use. Seek out tough linens in beautiful creams and naturals, or strong woven cottons in ticking, checked and striped designs. Experiment with bright plain

colours – blues, greens, pinks and orange. Explore the variety of warm woollen fibres, for use as upholstery, soft throws or insulating curtains. Bring the room alive with natural elements: light scented candles or soak up the warmth of a blazing fire.

Sitting rooms should be comfortable and relaxed rooms where you can sprawl out on a sofa with a good book, listen to music, watch the box, or simply sit back and think. Colour, comfort, texture and warmth are important factors in putting together an agreeable, functional space.

From curtains to loose covers, fabric colours can change a room as much as the impact of paint. Don't worry about slavishly matching the cushion cover, to the curtain lining, to the tie on your favourite slip cover. It is much more interesting to try out similar but contrasting fabric shades. I remember a room I decorated to a spring theme where creamy yellow walls contrasted with bright

right *Blue-and-white is fresh with decorative details like crisp striped cushions and scrunchy Roman blinds, faded floral loose covers, and lots of checked cotton accessories.*

below *French metal daybeds can be found in salesrooms and antique shops and look great with striped cotton ticking bolsters or plain white cushions or throws. Paint them white or leave them bare.*

Blues, greens and greys
are useful colour tools.
left *Powder blue
paintwork looks sharp
against bold navy striped
slip covers and cushions
in assorted shades of
blue cotton stripe. White
brickwork walls and
whitened parquet
flooring emphasize the
airy feel.*
far right *A painted grey
skirting adds subtle
definition to plain white
walls in a light and
fresh Provençal sitting
room. Reclaimed
terracotta tiles laid in
an uneven pattern
add to the
vernacular effect.*
right *Warming not cold:
rich blue-green emulsion
paint makes a distinctive
foil for white woodwork, a
plain white dustsheet
throw and polished
wooden floorboards.*

green-and-white checked blinds, together with loose covers in a dark cabbage-leaf colour and cushions in a lime green and thin blue-and-white striped cotton. The overall effect was bright, sunny and easy to live with.

Sitting rooms must be comfortable and this relies partly on well-made, sturdy upholstery. It is far more satisfactory to invest in a good-quality second-hand sofa, say, than something brand new, mass-produced and lightweight. I know an enterprising woman who sells everything from hand-me-down Knole sofas from stately homes to junk armchairs, all piled up in barns and outhouses in a farmhouse. If you invest in new upholstery test it out for comfort before buying: sit on it for ten minutes,

bounce up and down on the seat (you should be able to feel the underlying support); lean back (you should not feel any springs protruding from the framework); lift it to test the weight of the framework (it should not be too lightweight).

Upholstery fabric should be hard-wearing. Some of the best fabrics are linen and linen–cotton mixes. A few years ago I found some wonderful earthy coloured linen reduced at a fabric outlet, on sale at 15 per cent of the usual price. I bought up ten metres which was enough to cover a Victorian chesterfield. Despite heavy wear and tear from parties, children, dogs and cats it is still looking respectable, only of course I am now itching to find another bargain. Loose or slip covers are practical for cleaning and a budget way of updating

sofas and chairs. Loose covers can be made up with various details such as pleated or simple box skirts, self ties at the corners, or a row of buttons or a bow at the back. If you want a really instant update, cover up an unattractive sofa, perhaps in rented accommodation, with a white sheet or a simple check cotton throw. This is also a good idea for giving upholstery a change for the summer.

You can create a wonderful room with a great colour scheme and lots of decorative ideas, but if it's cold, it's miserable. The ultimate in warmth and atmosphere is a blazing log fire — and woods such as chestnut and apple give off delicious smoky scents. Ecologically sound but second-best is smokeless coal. Not everybody has access to wood, or the inclination to lay and maintain a real fire, so flame-effect fires are worth considering. Although they don't throw out as much heat as a real fire and inevitably look artificial, they are not a bad compromise. Underfloor heating schemes, common in Scandinavia and North America, involve hidden pipes connected to the central-heating system — a great way of dispensing with unsightly radiators.

Splashes of terracotta act as warming detail in the cream sitting room of a London Georgian town-house. Amongst furnishing and fabrics in blues, greens and yellows there is a kelim rug in faded earth and brick. Spread across the marble mantlepiece are old clay pots and a rosemary wreath. Other rich ingredients seen below include old wooden Spanish soup bowls filled with rag balls made of scraps of checked and striped cotton and an antique three-legged milking stool. Opposite, a fold-up butler's tray acts as a versatile display idea with a candlestick lamp and a jug of spring flowers.

Roman blind

MATERIALS

calico fabric

batten, 2 cm x 5 cm (¾ x 2 in) thick

brackets

Velcro tape

staple gun or tacks

pins

needle

thread

sewing machine

looped blind tape

lath, 3 cm (1½ in) wide

blind cord

eyelets (as many as there are rows of tape)

wall cleat with screws

Roman blinds are a simple and stylish window treatment for any room around the house and do not require massive amounts of fabric. For durability make blinds up in a tough fabric texture such as heavy canvas, linen or calico as in the creamy coloured example shown here, which has been self-lined to make it look smart from the outside.

MEASURING UP

1. Roman blinds can either hang outside the window frame so that the entire window frame is covered or, as illustrated here, they can fit neatly into a recess.

2. Measure the width and length of the window in order to calculate the amount of fabric you need. Cut two pieces of fabric each 9 cm (3½ in) wider and 11.5 cm (4½ in) longer than the window.

MAKING UP

1. To fit a Roman blind to the window it should be attached to a wooden batten, cut to fit the width of your window and hung from brackets fixed either side of the window frame.

2. I find it easier to take the blind down to clean it if it is secured to the batten by Velcro. Using either a staple gun or tacks, secure the toothed side of the Velcro to the top edge of the batten.

3. Take the two pieces of fabric and, with right sides facing, pin, baste and machine stitch them together along the two long edges and one of the short edges, using a seam allowance of 1 cm (½ in). Turn right side out and press.

4. Cut two pieces of ringed tape to the same length as the blind. The first ring should start 15 cm (6 in) from the

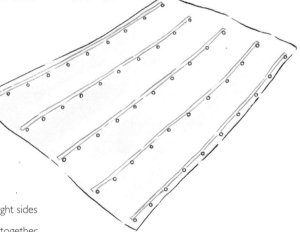

top of the blind. Pin these pieces of tape along each side of the blind, close to the edge, then machine stitch in place. Space the remaining tape evenly at approximately 30 cm (12 in) intervals. Check that the loops on all of the tapes are level across the width of the blind, and then cut the pieces to length and pin and machine stitch them in place.

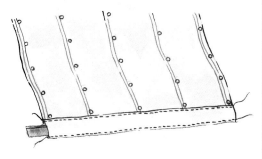

5. To finish the bottom edge, turn under 1 cm (½ in) and then 4 cm (1½ in), enclosing the ends of the tapes. Press and then machine stitch, taking care not to catch the loops whilst stitching. Machine stitch the hem close to the folded edge. Insert the lath into the casing to stiffen the blind and to help it to hang well. Secure the ends with hand stitching.

6. Turn the top of the blind over 1 cm (½ in) towards the tape. Pin, baste and machine stitch the other Velcro strip to this edge.

7. To calculate the amount of cord you need for each row of tape, measure twice the length of the blind plus one width. Tie one length of cord to the bottom ring of each row of tape and then thread the cord up through every loop in the tape to the top ring.

8. Fix an eyelet into the lower edge of the batten above each row of tape. Attach the blind to the batten with the Velcro and run the cords through the eyelets so that they all meet at the far left. Trim the cords to the same length and knot.

9. Fix the batten to the top of the window. Screw a cleat to the window frame so that the cords can be secured when the blind is pulled up.

this page *Neutral tones of white and cream create a peaceful feeling. Contemporary details include market finds such as a sixties basket chair and sunburst mirror, together with simple picture frames and streamlined lighting.*

far right *Harking back to fifties gum commercials, the owner of this cosy panelled sitting room in a traditional shingled house on Long Island aptly describes the subtly coloured paintwork as chewing-gum grey. Rough sisal matting, pine planking (resourcefully salvaged from packing crates) and neutrally coloured linen fabrics add to the fresh and understated effect.*

Cushions are important comfort factors. Buy proper feather or kapok-filled pads, as foam fillings are unsightly and lumpy. Pads squeezed into mean-sized covers don't look good, so make covers roomy and allow the cushion to 'breathe'. Simple piped cushions or flanged shapes are perennial classics. Bags with tie openings look good and are incredibly easy to run up on the sewing machine at home. You can make up cushions in just about any fabric – I like tough blue-and-white checked Indian cotton, striped ticking and light cotton in bright shades (which is good for a summery feel). You can also recycle covers from chopped-up old curtains, table cloths and off-cuts of fabric in your favourite colours or patterns. Anything faded and floral, especially blues and whites or soft pinks and lavenders will work well with checks, stripes and plains. If, say, you hanker after a beautiful floral cotton but can't afford the hefty price tag for a big soft furnishing project, then why not buy just half a metre, the average price of a pair of shoes, and make it up into a beautiful cushion for a favourite chair. It will last considerably longer than the shoes!

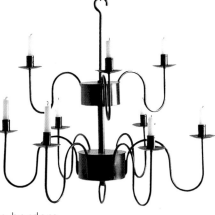

Deep-pile, wall-to-wall white carpet might be appropriate in a boudoir-like bedroom, but for everyday stylish living natural flooring textures such as coir, sisal, seagrass and cotton, or wool rugs in checks and stripes, are more liveable with in terms of cost and practicality. For insulation, layer rugs over one another. Buy mats that are bound with hessian or woven cotton borders as these look better and prevent fraying. Cotton rugs are cheap and many are designed to be thrown in the washing machine, but remember that very bright colours might run and so should be carefully hand washed. Thick tartan wool rugs are a good investment.

far left For a homespun feel with an updated edge this loft space has been decorated with pristine white walls, contemporary galvanized metal buckets and a primitive-style metal chandelier. Woven cotton bought in a sale has been used to make simple loose covers for a battered old sofa and chairs.

left More homespun ideas: disparate furniture from a sale is unified with soft grey paint.

Loose cover for a sofa

If you have an old sofa at home that's looking a bit worse for wear, don't get rid of it. Old sofas are usually far more solidly built than new ones, so it's worth giving it a fresh start. Complete re-upholstering can be very expensive, but this idea is cheap and simple.

MATERIALS

9 m (10 yds) pre-washed white cotton drill, (150 cm) 60 in wide
pins
tape measure
tailor's chalk
ruler
sewing machine

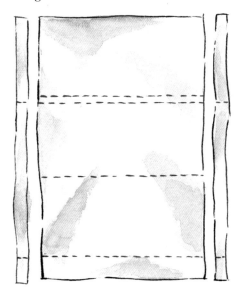

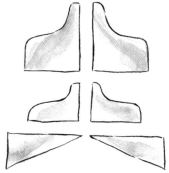

CUTTING AND MARKING THE FABRIC

1. Remove the cushions and mark a line down the centre of the sofa with pins, front and back as shown. Measure the total distance and add 7.5 cm (3 in) for hems; cut a piece of fabric to this length for the all-in-one back, seat and front piece.

2. Fold the fabric in half lengthways with right sides together and mark the fold line with tailor's chalk. Place this fold along the pinned centre line on the sofa, letting 3.5 cm (1½ in) hang down below both the front and the back. Open out the cloth and smooth it into place to cover the sofa, pushing it tightly into the corners. Pin it to the sofa along the existing seam lines on the original cover.

3. On this sofa, a 9 cm (3½ in) wide band runs up and over the arm and down the back of each side. To cut out the correct amount of fabric for these bands, measure this total length and add 7.5 cm (3 in) for hems. The width should be 12.5 cm (5 in). Pin the strips onto the sofa arms and down the back along the side seam lines, allowing a 3 cm (1½ in) seam allowance to hang down at both the front and the back. Using your chalk, mark a line where the front and the top of the back sections of the sofa meet the bands. This will be your reference for matching up the pieces when you are making up the cover.

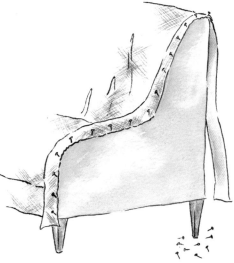

4. To cut the outside arm pieces fold the fabric in half and hold it against the side of the sofa, making sure the straight grain is vertical. Cut out the rough shape of the arm leaving a good 7.5 cm (3 in) seam allowance. Using the same method cut the inside arm shapes. Pin all four pieces right side down onto the sofa along the seam lines.

5. In between the side back and the back strip is a triangular gusset which allows the cover to slip easily on and off.

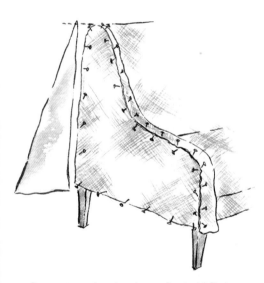

Cut out two triangular pieces of material. Each one should be 25 cm (10 in) at the widest point across the bottom. The height of the triangles should be equal to the height of the sofa back, plus 1.5 cm (¾ in) for the top seam allowance and 3 cm (1½ in) for the bottom hem. Join up these two points to form the triangles.

Mark three equidistant points down each side of the gussets for the ties. Put them to one side.

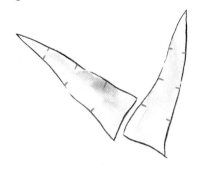

6. Mark the position of the seams with the tailor's chalk on all the sections following the pinned lines. Mark the junctions clearly with corresponding numbers so you know exactly which sections must be sewn together. Carefully remove the fabric and straighten the drawn seam lines with a ruler. Trim off all excess fabric leaving a uniform seam allowance of 1.5 cm (¾ in).

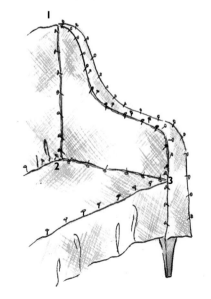

HOW TO MAKE THE COVER

1. To make the gusset ties, cut out two strips measuring 100 × 4 cm (40 × 1½ in). Divide each strip into six sections and cut again. For each tie turn under ½ cm (¼ in) along both the long and one short raw edge and press. Fold the ties in half lengthways with wrong sides together and machine stitch along the folded edges.

2. Attach the ties to the wrong side of the gusset at the points marked previously by machine stitching across their width.

3. Placing right sides together, machine stitch both inside arms to the sofa seat back and the seat.

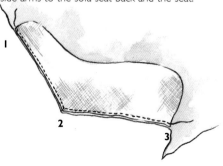

4. Machine stitch the bands to the inside arms and the main cover, right sides together, matching the marked seam lines and numbers.

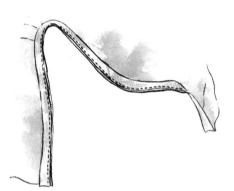

5. Next attach the outside arm sections to the band, with right sides facing, matching the seam lines and the corresponding numbers. Machine stitch the pieces together along the arm seam, but leave the back section open so that the gusset can be inserted.

At this stage, your sofa cover should look like this. The shape is now recognizable, but the back is still loose as the side gussets and ties have yet to be inserted.

6. Insert each gusset between the outside arm piece and the back section of the band and, with right sides together, stitch them in place.

7. At this stage, place the cover on the sofa to check the fit and length. The gusset will allow for a certain amount of flexibility; make any adjustments if necessary. Remove the cover and trim the seam allowances. Hem the bottom by turning under ½ cm (¼ in) followed by a further 1 cm (½ in) and stitching all round.

TO MAKE UP THE CUSHIONS

1. For two 69 × 61 × 10 cm (27½ × 24½ × 4 in) cushions, first cut out four rectangles measuring 72 × 64 cm (29 × 26 in) for the seat.

2. For the sides cut two strips of fabric measuring 194 × 13 cm (78 × 5 in) and for the backs cut two strips 72 × 16 cm (29 × 7 in), each of which must then be cut in half along the length.

3. Make up some ties as for the gusset. Allow six for each cushion and mark their positions on the opening edges of the back sections. Press under ½ cm (¼ in), followed by 1 cm (½ in) on these edges. Place the short raw edge of the ties under this turning and stitch along the length of the back opening through all layers close to the edge.

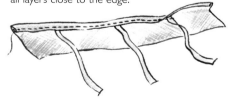

4. For each cushion, place the two back pieces together with the hemmed edges meeting and, with right sides together, stitch the side strip to both ends of the back section, using a seam allowance of 1 cm (½ in).

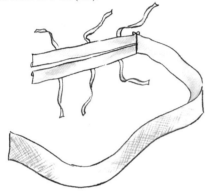

5. Mark the corner positions on each strip and turn them wrong side out; line up the top and bottom seat rectangles with these marks and pin, baste and machine stitch them in place with right sides together, using a 1 cm (½ in) seam allowance.

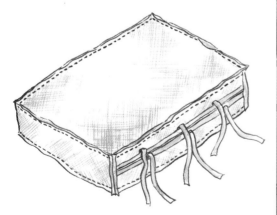

6. Trim the corners, turn the covers inside out, pull through the ties and insert the cushion pads.

Textures help determine the style and look of a room. Country cottage sitting rooms need rustic injections of rough wool throws, wood floors, tough sisal mats and hand-woven log baskets. Streamlined contemporary settings need smooth touches, such as slip covers in crisp white cotton, which help unify mismatched chairs and also complement pale wood floors. Modern materials such as zinc and aluminium for lighting and table surfaces also emphasize a more up-to-date look.

Curtains require substantial amounts of fabric but needn't break the bank. Stick to simple headings such as loops and ties. Choose strong cottons and linens. If you buy ten metres or more from many fabric wholesalers they will

left *Comfortable yet functional living spaces with seating covered in robust ticking or calico.*
below *A small space set aside for a home study area successfully houses vital office elements, including a basic trestle table, a metal filing cabinet, cheap cardboard box files revamped with paint and a smart metal twenties-style desk light.*

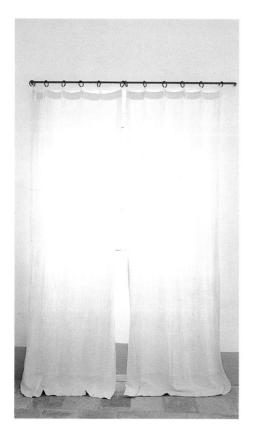

right Fresh and filmy: soft cream-coloured linen curtains with a decorative double-layered heading, recycled by the owner from a previous apartment. The wooden pole and rings are painted to create a unifying effect.

Simple shapes in plain fabrics create light and airy window treatments:
above *Light cotton curtains draped to the floor. They are simply tied onto a metal pole, bought by the length and bent over at the ends.*
right *Heavy canvas with eyelets can be hooked onto a window frame and pulled back as required.*

give you a substantial discount. Line curtains for a better hang and also to give protection from sunlight to prevent fading. Interlinings give greater insulation; bump is the thickest and looks like a blanket, while domette is a brushed cotton and the most commonly used. Roman or roller blinds are useful for providing extra insulation with curtains, as well as protecting from the sun (see the project on pages 100–101). Blinds also suit just about any window shape. I like Roman blinds and have examples in checked cotton and plain calico hanging at my Georgian sash windows; these are all hand washable in the bath. Unlined curtains in filmy textures such as muslin and organdie are cheap, stylish options. If you live in a climate with hot summers and cold winters, have sets of light curtains for summer and warmer pairs of thermal ones for winter, as you do for underwear. Paint curtain poles the same colour as walls for a unifying effect. Very cheap ideas for poles include wooden dowelling from timber yards cut to length and painted, and stretchy wire which is ideal for small drops, for example in cottage windows, and available from hardware and DIY shops

Pot pourri

The wood shavings and dried flowers in many shop-bought pot pourris are no match for the simple scented examples you can make yourself. It is easy to dry garden flower petals, herbs and citrus fruit slices and peels. For scent, use drops of deliciously fragrant essential oils and contain the smell with a fixative such as orris root or cloves. Alternatively buy ready-made oil blends from herbal and pot pourri specialists or read books on the subject to create your own subtle tailor-made examples.

MATERIALS

china bowl for mixing
seal or lid for bowl
wooden spoon

SUMMER FLOWER POT POURRI INGREDIENTS

125 g (4 oz) lavender flowers and stems, pinks flower heads, delphinium petals, rose petals, hydrangea petals, and any other garden flower petals you can glean
15 g (½ oz) orris root powder
20 drops geranium oil

HERBY POT POURRI INGREDIENTS

50 g (2 oz) bay leaves
50 g (2 oz) rosemary cut into 15 cm (6 in) lengths
15 g (½ oz) whole cloves
20 drops rosemary oil

ORANGE AND LEMON POT POURRI INGREDIENTS

500 g (1 lb) oranges
500 g (1 lb) lemons
8 whole clementines
25 drops orange oil

SUMMER FLOWER POT POURRI

My mother makes this every year with as many petals and flower heads as she can collect from her garden in the summer. The faded colours give it an old-fashioned country garden effect, and it is good to have a reminder of the summer borders to carry through the winter months.

INSTRUCTIONS

1. To dry the flowers, stems and petals spread them thinly on several sheets of newspaper on flat trays. Make sure none of the flowers overlaps another. Leave the trays in an airing cupboard or similar warm dark dry place until all of the flowers are thoroughly dried out.

2. Using a china bowl to avoid staining and a wooden spoon, mix the dried ingredients with the orris root powder. Take care not to damage the dried flowers which will now be very brittle. Add the oil and mix again. Seal the bowl for at least four weeks to allow the fragrances to fully develop and then transfer the pot pourri to your favourite dishes and containers.

HERBY POT POURRI

I like the sludgy green colours of this aromatic mixture. It looks lovely in white china or wooden bowls on a sideboard or kitchen dresser. Even when dried, the bay leaves retain a little of their fresh scent, and the herby effect is enhanced with the addition of fragrant rosemary oil. For an even prettier effect, pick some of the rosemary stems with the flowers still on them.

INSTRUCTIONS

1. Lay the bay leaves and the rosemary stems onto seveal sheets of newspaper laid on flat trays, taking care that the leaves and stems do not touch. Place the trays in an airing cupboard or similar warm dry dark space and leave them until the herbs are completely dried.

2. Mix the dried herbs with the cloves in the china bowl, using the wooden spoon. Take care not to damage the brittle bay leaves. Add the rosemary oil and then mix again. Seal the bowl for at least four weeks to allow the herbs to absorb the oil and then transfer the mix to your chosen containers.

ORANGE AND LEMON POT POURRI

Slices of dried citrus fruits scented with orange oil look and smell earthy and organic.

INSTRUCTIONS

1. Thinly peel the oranges and lemons and retain the strips of peel. Carefully slice the whole fruits into circles. Make incisions in the peel of the clementines, making sure that the whole fruit remains intact. Lay everything on sheets of newspaper in an airing cupboard or warm place until thoroughly dry.

2. Mix the fruit in the bowl with the wooden spoon. Add the orange oil. Mix again. Seal the bowl for at least four weeks and then transfer to containers; shallow bowls are best because the slices can then be arranged in layers.

Sleeping in style

We do so much of it that sleep deserves to be a peaceful and luxuriating experience. On a cold winter's night it is bliss to curl up in crisp white bedlinen and warm woolly blankets. Conversely, in summer it's good to lie with the sparest of bedclothes, say just a fine cotton sheet, and an open window to catch a cooling night-time breeze. Bedrooms need to be quiet airy refuges away from domestic distractions. There should be lots of cupboards, boxes or ample wardrobe space to stow away clothing and clutter. Some of the best ideas include capacious built-in walk-in wardrobes with simple panelled doors. Old laundry baskets, big wooden boxes and even old shoe boxes covered in fabric and paint are also useful bedroom storage notions. Bedroom textures need to be soft and inviting, such as filmy muslin curtains, plain calico blinds and fine cotton pyjamas. Soft wool blankets in creams or blues are great for dressing beds. Then there are antique quilts with pretty floral sprigged designs, that look lovely folded or draped over a bedstead. Spend as much as you can afford on bedding — soft goosedown duvets and pillows are the ultimate bedtime luxury. It is also prudent to invest in a well-sprung mattress.

A bedroom is a sanctuary, away from work and other people; it is a place where you can tuck yourself up in between crisp sheets with a good book to read, a drink, and a bar of chocolate. Asleep or not, all of us spend so much time there that it should be the one room in the house where we can be indulgent. Bedroom textures should be luxurious, soft and warm. The stresses of the day fall away when you clamber into white cotton sheets, curl up under soft blankets and hug a comforting hot water bottle in cold weather. It pays to invest in the best bedding you can afford and take time in choosing the right bed.

There are all sorts of bed shapes to suit the look you want to achieve. At a basic level there is a divan which can be dressed quite simply, useful in bedrooms that double up as daytime sitting rooms or studies.

Comfort factors in bed-rooms include freshly laundered sheets and warm creamy coloured wool blankets. Trawl markets and second-hand shops for old bedlinen; the quality is often better than modern textures. Really worth looking out for are old damask bed covers and fine embroidered linen pillowcases. Sleep peacefully in a traditional bedstead: classic brass always looks wonderful, and decorative ironwork looks great painted white. Create an oasis of calm with a clutter-free room.

119

MATERIALS

metal chair

tape measure

pattern paper

pencil and pen

pins

scissors

striped cotton

needle

thread

sewing machine

Slip cover for a metal chair

A simple metal chair can be totally transformed with a lick of white paint and a tied slip cover. Here a fresh blue-and-white striped washable cotton is tailored to the shape of the chair so that it retains its gently curved outline. For added detail you could sew a row of contrasting buttons down the back seam.

HOW TO MAKE UP

1. First measure the three parts of the chair to be covered: the seat (A), the inside back (B) and the outside back (C). Transfer the dimensions of A, B and C onto pattern paper, adding a 1.25 cm (½ in) seam allowance all round. On pattern A mark the positions of the two rear chair legs with a cross. Take the outside back panel (C) and cut it in half vertically so splitting the pattern in two, then add a 1.25 cm (½ in) seam allowance to each new straight edge; this will form an opening at the back of the chair so that the cover can be easily slipped on and also removed. Using the paper patterns just made, cut out all four pieces in the striped fabric, making sure that you keep the direction of the stripes consistent.

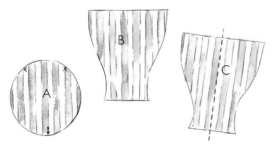

2. For the frill, measure around the perimeter of the front of the chair seat from one rear leg to the other. Multiply this measurement by three.

3. Cut out a strip of fabric 15 cm (6 in) wide and stitch together strips to the required length, as measured in the previous step. Turn under the bottom edge and sides of the strip, pin, baste and machine stitch, leaving the top edge for gathering. With contrasting thread make gathers along the top edge so that the frill fits the edge of the front of the seat.

4. When the strip is gathered, align the arrow marked above with the arrow marked on pattern A. Pin, baste and machine stitch the gathered frill to the front perimeter of piece A, right sides facing.

5. To make the ties, cut out two strips of fabric, each 2.5 cm (1 in) wide and 17 cm (7 in) long. Fold each in half lengthways with right sides facing. Machine stitch along a short and a long edge, turn right side out through the open end and hand sew to a neat close. The finished tie should be about 1.25 cm (½ in) wide. Repeat for the second tie and press. In the same way make two shorter ties each 2.5 cm (1 in) wide.

6. Position one of the longer ties centrally over a cross marked on piece A, indicating the position of the rear chair legs. Sew firmly in place (see below). Repeat for the second longer tie.

7. Place two halves of C right sides together and stitch one third of the way down, forming a central seam. Turn in, pin and hand sew all the remaining raw edges. Place pieces B and C right sides facing. Pin, baste and machine stitch along both the sides and the top and then turn right side out.

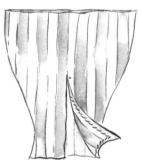

8. To complete the frill, cut out a strip 15 cm (6 in) wide and three times the length of seat edge between the two rear legs. Cut the strip in half. Turn under the bottom and side edges, pin and machine stitch leaving the top edges for gathering.

9. Stitch the gathered frills, right sides together, to the bottom edges of piece C. Attach the remaining ties to the rear opening to fasten.

10. Pin, baste and machine stitch the bottom edge of panel B to the back edge of piece A, right sides facing. Press, slip over the chair and fasten the ties.

below *Grey paintwork and a simple painted bedside table, together with a subtlely checked blue woollen blanket and a glass of vibrant yellow spring daffodils, add colourful injections to the overall neutral effect created by the white walls and bedlinen in this restful Provençal farmhouse bedroom.*

right *Brilliant blues lend a seaside air to a Long Island bedroom. Blue-and-white patchwork quilts, boldly striped cotton pillowcases, and white painted walls add to the bright and breezy feel, while a faded denim child's sailor suit hung on the wall brings a jaunty touch to the coastal theme.*

I prefer bright and airy bedrooms in whites and creams, in other words rooms that have a light ambience throughout the year. Darker, richer colours such as library green or study red may suit some individuals, but waking up to moody walls on dark mornings during a long winter may quickly become a gloomy prospect. Bedrooms need to be comfortable, optimistic places, with supplies of good reading matter, soft bedside lighting, some sort of seating, and maybe a jug of favourite scented flowers.

There is nothing to beat the simplicity of plain white bedlinen. It is smart and unassuming. When an injection of colour is desired then you can look to bold, contemporary designs, perhaps in tomato red, lime green, fuchsia pink or lemon yellow. These sorts of bedlinens work particularly well in southern climates with strong light. It seems that English country-house style with its fussy floral patterned sheets and pillowcases have had their day on the decoration scene (and not too soon). But at the mass-market end of things manufacturers persist in launching frilly, flowery designs that make beds look like the covers of chocolate boxes. However, florals in the bedroom can look really pretty, if used carefully and with restraint. Take as an example a simple lavender-coloured country bedroom theme, suitable say for a cottage bedroom. You can make up basic pillowcases in a delicate rose-bud print (note that dress fabrics often have more subtle floral designs than their furnishing counterparts) and combine with white sheets and pillowcases and a faded antique floral patchwork quilt. Stick to a plain cotton window treatment, paint the walls white and cover the floors in cheap, neutral cotton rugs. The whole effect is stylish and not in the least bit overdone or too pretty.

left *A romantic mahogany* bateau lit *is a great vehicle for layer upon layer of wonderful white antique bedlinen. A filmy mosquito net, functional as well as decorative, is generously swathed from the ceiling to complete the translucent effect.*

right *Distinctive in texture and colour, smooth polished parquet flooring and bentwood furniture are smart, dark contrasts to creamy walls and bedlinen in a Paris flat.*

Forced to make my bed from an early age, I think that an orderly, uncluttered bedroom helps to set you up mentally for whatever difficulties and chaos you may come across during the day. Storage, of course, is a key issue. It is quite surprising how a few pieces of casually flung clothing, or perhaps a modest pile of discarded newspapers, is all it takes to create a bedroom scene that begins to look like a jumble sale. A built-in run of shelves with doors along one wall is a very successful way of stowing away clothes, hats, shoes, bags, suitcases and other unavoidable clutter. Free-standing armoires and wardrobes are useful, but impractical if space is tight. If you are restricted to a limited budget then you can curtain off an alcove with calico, linen or even an old bedspread. Save for a couple of hours spent at the sewing machine,

the results are almost instantaneous and very stylish. A large chest of drawers is always useful for swallowing up smaller items of clothing and spare bedlinen. Old trunks, big boxy laundry baskets and modern-looking zinc boxes are also useful bedroom storage devices.

Bedsteads offer a variety of decorative possibilities. A Shaker-style painted wooden four-poster frame looks good with tie-on curtains, a muslin or linen pelmet, or left entirely bare. Good value examples are available in flat-pack kit form. Nineteenth-century French metal daybeds are excellent for bed-sitting rooms and look really smart with ticking bolsters and pillows; they are not difficult to find if you track down dealers who specialize in antique French decorative furniture. If you have children in the family then consider pine bunk beds. Available from most department stores or large furniture warehouses, they are very good value and can be dressed up with a coat of paint.

Those of us who enjoy the pleasures of a firm bed know high-quality bedding really does help towards getting a good night's sleep. The best type of mattress is sewn to size

right A country feel is evoked by matt-painted panelling, wood boards, a painted wooden bed, and simple fabrics and furnishings in a Georgian townhouse. An antique lavender patch-work quilt with a seaweed design and pink sprigged floral pillowcases, run up in lawn dress fabric, provide fresh detail.

left *Hot shots: vivid splashes of bright colour work well in sunny, southern climates. Experiment with cool cotton bedlinen in bold blues, greens, yellows, pinks and orange. As temperatures soar, practical ideas for keeping cool are essential: windows flung wide let air flow through, light muslin curtains help to catch a breeze and stone floor tiles stay cool underfoot.*

with layers of white curled feather, together with fleece wool and white cotton felt all incorporated with solid box springs. Perfect pillows are combinations of duck down and feather, grey duck feather, or the ultimate luxury, white goose feather. And for people with allergies there are special hog and cattle hair versions available. It is well worth your while spending that little bit more when it comes to buying bedding, both for increased comfort and longevity.

My dream is to sleep in daily pressed and laundered linen sheets. Until this fantasy is realized I remain content with a box of assorted cotton linens at various stages of wear and tear. My softest sheets are in Egyptian cotton, bought years ago, and still going strong. I also love antique bedlinen and have various Victorian linen and cotton lace pillowcases, as well as the odd linen sheet handed down from elderly relatives, or bought in junk shops and markets. Although pure linen sheets are very costly, and need extra care and maintenance, they will last a lifetime. When buying linen it should feel clean, starched, crisp and tightly woven. Modern linens shed creases faster than traditional ones, reducing the sweat of ironing.

Duvets have become an almost universal item of bedding, but sheets and blankets have been making a bit of a comeback recently. The practical thing about layers of bed clothes is that you can simply peel back or pull on the layers to suit the temperature. In summer, for example, a cotton blanket and sheet are all that is necessary and if the temperature suddenly plummets then there is nothing to beat the addition of a traditional wool blanket with a satin ribbon binding.

below *Bunk beds are an economical and useful idea for children's bedrooms and are popular for their space-saving qualities as well as being fun to sleep in. Update and give a stylish look to plain pine bunks with pale eggshell paint as seen here.*

Clean living

To start the day, an invigorating shower, or simply a wash in a basin of hot water, wakes you up and triggers circulation. At other times, and especially at the end of the day, I can spend hours soaking in a tub of steaming hot water listening to the radio (sneaking off for a mid-afternoon session is also highly recommended for a rare treat). They may not be the best at conserving heat but smooth cast-iron baths are definitely the most agreeable to soak in. It's good to scent the water with fragrant oil or work up a creamy lather with soap. A bleached wooden bath rack is a useful vehicle for storing soaps and flannels and keeping reading material dry and readily to hand. Loofahs, sponges and brushes are also essential bathroom tools for keeping skin pristine and well scrubbed. To accompany daily washing rituals, use fluffy towels in white, seaside blues and bright spring green colours. Soft towelling bathrobes are also a delicious way of drying off — buy big sizes for wrapping up

well. The best showers soak you with a powerful delivery, and have finely tuned taps that deliver hot or cold water as you require it. Keep bathrooms well ventilated to clear steam, and invest in duck-boards and bathmats to mop up pools of water.

A bath, a shower, or even a quick face splash are instant revivers and help relieve the stresses of daily living. Like eating, washing can be a deliciously sensual ritual. It can vary from a short, sharp, invigorating cold outdoor shower on a hot summer's day to a more languid experience in mid-winter when a long, hot, steaming bath is the perfect antidote to dark days and icy temperatures. Copious supplies of hot water are at the top of my list of crucial bathroom ingredients – even the meanest, most poky, drab little bathroom can be acceptable if it delivers piping-hot water, and plenty of it. Smelly soaps and lotions are essential elements too. Among my favourites are delicately scented rosewater soap and rose geranium bath gel. If I'm in the mood for more pungent aromas, I choose stronger-scented spicy soaps with warming tones.

White bathrooms are bright, light and airy, as shown by the gleaming examples seen here. Walls and woodwork are in varying shades of white together with pristine clean ceramic tiles, baths and sinks. Deliciously tactile textures include big fluffy towels, soft sponges and tough cottons for laundry bags.

Bathroom wall cabinet

Give a basic pine bathroom cabinet a new look with seaside-inspired greeny blue paint, and a utilitarian but stylish chicken wire front. You can apply the same treatment to any old cupboard picked up in a market or junk shop.

MATERIALS

wall cabinet
pin hammer
white spirit
steel wool
fine grade sandpaper
primer
undercoat
eggshell paint
2.5 cm (1 in) paint brush
chicken wire from a hardware shop
wire cutters
staple gun or panel pins

HOW TO MAKE UP

1. Choose a cabinet that has a single central panel in the door. If it is an old cabinet make sure that the door construction is sound. Remove any beading holding the panel in place on the the inside of the door and then carefully knock out the panel by tapping around the edge with a pin hammer. Avoid damaging any beading around the front of the panel by knocking through from the front. If the cabinet has a mirror or glass in the door panel, remove the pins holding the glass in place and then very carefully push it out.

2. Prepare all surfaces before painting to ensure they are in the best possible condition. If the cabinet has been waxed, remove the wax coating with white spirit and steel wool, then clean with a rag. Always work in the direction of the grain. If it has been painted before and the paintwork is sound simply wash it down and sand it. If the old paint is chipped or flaking it is better to strip it off.

3. Apply a coat of primer, then one of undercoat, followed by two coats of eggshell. It is important to sand with a fine grade sandpaper between each coat to give a smooth surface for the next one.

Remember to paint all of the inside surfaces as well as they will be visible through the chicken wire; painting the shelves a contrasting colour, as here, is a smart idea.

4. Cut your chicken wire to size using wire cutters. Attach the wire to the reverse side of the cabinet door frame with a staple gun or panel pins bent over to catch the edges of the wire.

CLEAN LIVING

right *Real forties bathrooms were cold clammy places with peeling linoleum floors and intermittent hot water issued from unpredictable gas boilers. The sea green and white Long Island bathroom here might be retro in feeling, but is very modern in its comforting supplies of heat and hot water. Simple and functional, it houses a sturdy cast-iron bath on ball-and-claw feet, a plain wooden mirrored bath cabinet and a painted stool for resting a bathtime drink. Seek out ideas for recreating this relaxed, utilitarian look by rummaging around in second-hand shops for big white clinical enamel jugs (the sort that hospitals used for washing babies), old formica-topped tables, metal buckets and medicine cabinets, or old versions of the wooden bathmat below.*

Indispensible for drying off big white cotton bath sheets and white rag-rug Portuguese bath mats is my thirties-style heated chrome towel rail. To finish off the ablutions it's good to wrap up in a soft, white waffle cotton dressing gown — they're rather expensive, but well worth it for a daily dose of luxury.

Choosing a bath is a question of taste as well as practical considerations. Traditional-style, free-standing cast-iron baths with ball and claw feet are deep and look good but they do need sturdy floors to support their own weight, the considerable weight of a bathful of water, plus the weight of the bather. In contrast, modern acrylic baths are light, warm to the touch and come in lots of shapes.

above *More luxurious yet eminently achievable bathroom ideas include a tinkly glass candelabra for bathing by candle-light, and a comfy chair with soft towelling seat-ing. Practical bathroom storage ideas include woven cane laundry baskets and junk objects like old metal school shoe lockers or tin boxes used to house soaps, lotions and other paraphernalia.*

Drawstring bag

A basic bag shape can be made up in tough cotton and used to store everything from sewing materials to towels. The pattern shown here can be adapted to make roomy laundry bags, or sized down to make a trio of practical storage bags for the bathroom. If you want to be really organized you can label utility calico storage bags with indelible fabric pens.

MATERIALS

90 cm (37 in) heavy cotton, 115 cm (45 in) wide

tape measure

pins

scissors

needle

thread

safety pins

sewing machine

HOW TO MAKE UP

1. For the bag, cut out one piece of fabric measuring 92 x 42 cm (37 x 17 in). Fold the fabric in half, with right sides together, and pin, baste and machine stitch one of the long sides for 36 cm (14 in), using a seam allowance of 1 cm (½ in). Leave a 2 cm (¾ in) gap and then continue sewing to the end of the seam.

If you want to make a double tie repeat this process on the other long side. For a single tie follow these instructions for one long side only and machine a continuous line of stitching up the other long side. Press the seams open.

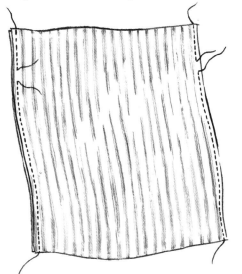

2. To make the casement that will contain the ties, fold over the top raw edge 1 cm (½ in) all round and press the fold in place. Then fold over a further 5 cm (2 in) evenly all round, lining up the side seams. Press and pin in position.

Machine stitch all round the top of the bag 1.5 cm (¾ in) from the folded edge. Make a second row of stitching around the bag 3 cm (1¼ in) below the first row. Make sure the line of stitches runs through the folded edge on the underside. Turn the bag right side out and press.

3. To make the ties, cut two strips of fabric 3 x 110 cm (1½ x 44 in). Turn under ½ cm (¼ in) on all four raw edges on each strip. Fold the strips in half lengthways and, with wrong sides facing, pin, baste and machine stitch along the open ends and side, close to the edge.

4. Attach a safety pin to one end of a tie and guide the tie through one of the casement holes, completing the full circle.

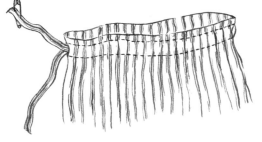

Repeat for the second tie, starting and finishing at the opposite hole. Remove the safety pins, knot the ties and pull the ends to draw.

far right *Get the look and create your own Georgian-inspired bathroom with sludgy matt eggshell paint, an old-fashioned bath on a raised platform and big weathered brass taps. Hide elements of contemporary life behind plain panelled cupboards. Seal wooden floors in matt varnish or use thick cotton bathmats to soak up water from dripping bodies.*

Enamelled steel baths are strong and hardwearing (and for this reason favoured by hotels and hospitals) but, like modern acrylic baths, they need the support of a frame. For stylish details either box in the bath with plain white tiles, or make a surround of tongue-and-groove wood panels which can be painted or waxed for protection.

Bathroom textures and surfaces need to be hardwearing and easy to maintain. Cleaning the bathroom

this page *Old ceramic jugs, weathered wooden shelves with cut-out patterns, cheap painted peg rails and seashell prints are key elements for a traditional feel.*

right *Daily ablutions are
an uplifting experience in
this bright and cheery sea
green and blue theme.
Solid functional fittings
that were happily left
intact for the owner
included a splendid old
ceramic sink on a stand
with classic taps and
visible fittings.*

The average bathroom showroom stocks a pretty paltry selection of taps and unremarkable shapes often cost the earth. Here are some inspiring ideas.
above *A single stainless steel spout with an artfully concealed tap mechanism.*
above right *Brass taps from a builder's yard.*
right *Chunky Victorian pillar taps found in a London salvage yard.*

becomes much less of a chore if you wipe down baths, washbasins and showers daily with soapy water while they are still warm, then rinse and dry; this helps prevent a build-up of dirt. Try not to use abrasive cleaners which can damage many surfaces and glazes; choose softer sponges or cloths instead.

Ceramic sinks, basins, lavatories and shower trays are widely available, and good value. Ceramic tiles for floors and walls provide a good splash-proof environment. Wooden floors are acceptable if well sealed, as is terra-cotta, or even linoleum, provided it is properly laid to stop water seeping underneath and causing damp. Avoid carpet

this page *Introduce colour to bathrooms with bright towels and marine-blue and lime-green robes or deep blue glass bottles for lotions and potions.*

far right *Swimming-pool inspired tiny blue mosaic tiles are an inventive idea for a walk-in shower space. Equally resourceful are basic stainless steel kitchen mixer taps reinvented as shower taps and spouts.*

as sooner or later it will get wet, and begin to turn mouldy and smelly.

When planning a shower it is essential to check that you have enough water pressure to produce a powerful downpour. You might need a pump that automatically boosts the flow. Showers can be simple affairs — from a hand set fitted to the bath taps with a protective screen or curtain, to a state-of-the-art walk-in room with a shower that delivers deluges of water.

There are numerous ways of storing bathroom equipment. Built-in cupboards are useful and one which houses a boiler will make practical airing-cupboard space for keeping hot, dry towels to hand. Boxes and baskets are good for stowing away dirty linen, spare towels or bathroom brushes and sponges. Versatile peg racks in wood and metal are ideal for hanging up sponge bags and flannels.

Outdoor living

When the temperature rises and the days lengthen images of summer reappear: like sand between the toes, warm bare skin, icy drinks and creased cool linen, and it's time to head outside. Dedicated lovers of the outdoors will already have grabbed the pleasures of those first few tentative days of spring when it's a revelation to feel and see the sun again after months of dreary winter. They pack up picnic baskets and rugs and head off for the first coast or countryside excursion of the season. Given a sunny day and appropriate clothing I will pack up a thermos of hot soup, smoked salmon and cream cheese bagels and head off with my family to an empty stretch of south coast beach.

Then, when summer is well established there is that feeling that it will go on forever and everyone becomes complacent and even irritated with the heat and humidity. But what luxury when the days are long and the evenings balmy to eat breakfast, lunch, tea or supper *al fresco*.

Invigorating as well as relaxing, the event can be as simple as a coffee taken at a pavement café – something blissful for gardenless city dwellers – or a weekend picnic in the park with friends, sharing the best cheese, bread and wine affordable.

Eating outside is one of life's sensual pleasures. Whatever the scenario, from a windswept beach beneath racing clouds to a warm jasmine-scented Mediterranean night, food seems to develop in taste and texture when eaten out in the elements. The British, for instance, have always been keen on picnics, packing up thermos flasks, rugs, raincoats and quantities of ham sandwiches to face unpredictable weather with determination. In complete contrast, the southern Spaniards give in to fiercely hot summer afternoons and laze around shady tables idling over *jamón*, bread, wine and steaming paellas cooked up on portable primus stoves.

The passion for eating *al fresco* has grown with me into adult life. Childhood picnics are remembered for their delicious informality, where for once adults didn't bother with cutlery or insist on elbows being off the table, or even mind if you sprawled sandwich in hand. In summer, inspired by books such as Elizabeth David's *Summer Cooking*, my picnics might include baguettes soaked with olive oil and garlic, stuffed with goats' cheese and anchovies. All this is stored in one of those not very sightly, but eminently practical, plastic cool boxes, together with drinks of beer, bubbly Cava or crisp dry Manzanilla sherry.

At home my tiny backyard becomes an extra room in summer. There is not much sun, but climbing roses and clematis manage to thrive, and flower pots filled with herbs add colour, texture and culinary detail. As soon as the temperature allows, we set up a big wooden table and green metal folding chairs. I like to spread the table with white or blue-and-white check cloths together with jars of nasturtiums or cow parsley. In the evening, candles set in pots provide a wonderful glow and they don't blow out.

left *Keep cool with a shady awning made from sheets of cane spread over a simple iron framework. Other ideas for retreating out of the sun include panels of striped or plain canvas stretched hammock-style across a small courtyard, patio or between trees. For a more permanent arrangement that can be stored over the winter months, invest in a big canvas umbrella on metal or wooden frames. I've seen good ones in basic green-and-white stripes, designed for use on the beach but equally at home in the back garden or country.*

The only rule for food served outside is that is should be delicious and easy to eat.

Junk furniture

table

chairs

fine grade sandpaper

wire wool

white spirit

hardboard

primer

undercoat

eggshell paint

2.5 cm (1 in) paint brush

cotton roller towel fabric

cotton tape

Just about any old junk furniture can be given a facelift with a coat of paint and some simple covers. I found two wooden chairs and a very battered card table in a local street market and spruced them up with brilliant white eggshell.

INSTRUCTIONS

1. Prepare the table and chair surfaces for painting by sanding with fine grade sandpaper. If they have been waxed, clean with white spirit and wire wool, then clean with a rag, always working in the direction of the grain. If they have been painted before and are in good condition then just wash them down, dry and sand. If the old paint is flaking or chipped it is best to strip it off.

2. The card table was bought with a felt top and so I replaced it with a piece of hardboard, cut to size and pinned to the frame.

3. Apply primer then undercoat, followed by two coats of eggshell. To ensure a smooth surface for the next coat of paint, rub down with fine sandpaper after each coat is dry.

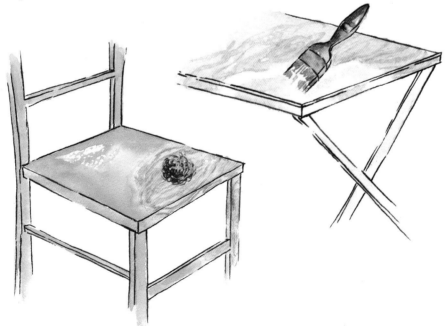

4. To make almost instant covers I used lengths of cotton roller towel which comes in finished narrow widths. This fabric is ideal since it is designed for commercial use and will withstand lots of wear and frequent washing. Measure your lengths so that the cover hangs 15 cm (6 in) below the seat at the back and front. Fray each of the short ends to 2.5 cm (1 in) and sew four lengths of tape 15 cm (6 in) long to the towel at the points where the seat meets the back. Drape the finished cover over the chair and tie the tapes to secure it in place.

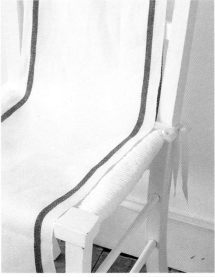

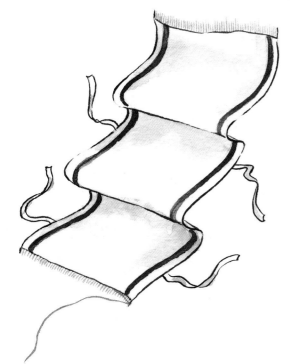

left *Durable, portable and attractive outdoor ideas: folding wooden tables and chairs (these were borrowed from the local village bar in Spain but similar ones can be found in second-hand furniture shops); lengths of cotton for tablecloths, cushions for comfort; bright yellow plastic tumblers; woven olive baskets; and jars packed with freshly picked herbs for decoration.*

When I am able to visit a good fishmonger we eat barbecued salmon steaks, sardines, or mackerel stuffed with parsley, lemon and garlic. For pudding I sometimes make strawberry or raspberry ice cream with the help of a small electric ice cream machine, and serve it with summer berries and hunks of shortbread.

Equipment for eating out in the open has never been so varied. Chain stores stock bright plastic picnic kits that are great value. Sleek, streamlined and shatter-proof stainless flasks that keep fluids hot or cold are also useful. Furniture ideas include fold-up slatted chairs that can be stowed away easily in winter. If your funds don't run to an expensive garden table then cheat with an old door laid across trestles, and cover it with a cloth in a favourite fabric.

Credits

154

crates painted in Colour World E9-23 green J.W. Bollom; laundry basket Tobias and the Angel; blanket Melin Tregwynt; blue and green cotton fabric The Conran Shop; storage chest Ikea; boxes Habitat painted in pottery JWB86, J.W. Bollom; peg rail Ikea

page 59 *clockwise from top*: glass storage jars Divertimenti; pine cupboard Ikea painted in blue eggshell; butchers hooks Divertimenti; buckets The Conran Shop and hardware stores; galvanized steel storage boxes Muji; shoe rack Ikea; beaker Muji; clothes rail B.S. Sales; shoe boxes fabric Manuel Canovas

page 60 picture frames Ikea

page 61 plates English Country Antiques, USA; picture frames Habitat; pudding basins Divertimenti; shadow boxes Habitat

page 62 *clockwise from top*: mug Habitat; tartan plate Anta; white coffee cup and saucer Habitat; blue-and-white china Crate & Barrel, USA; dinner plate Heal's; Champagne flute The Conran Shop; Duralex tumbler Spanish supermarket; ripple glass Designers Guild; tumbler Crate & Barrel, USA; tumbler Pottery Barn, USA; Misu tumbler Ikea; Cornishware plate Heal's

page 63 *clockwise from top*: gingham bowl McCord; jug Divertimenti; blue-and-white bowl Habitat; spotty bowl Designers Guild; cream cup and saucer by Veronique Pichon at Designers Guild; white plate Wedgwood; Poole pottery jug Designers Guild.

pages 66–67 enamel jug Ruby Beets Antiques, USA

pages 68–69 saucepans Brick Lane Market; tartan plates Anta; sink and taps Aston Matthews

pages 70–71 Swedish stove Jotul; interior design Susie Manby; trug Clifton Nurseries

pages 72–73 tins painted in Farrow & Ball 44 cream eggshell; crates painted in Colour World E6-46 (yellow) J.W. Bollom, Colour World E9-23 (green) J.W. Bollom, Pottery JWB86 (blue) J.W. Bollom; flower pots painted in White matt emulsion J.W. Bollom and vinyl matt emulsion Lavender Lave 21-17 Sanderson Spectrum

pages 74–75 Kilner jars After Noah; cake tins Brick Lane Market; white metal chair Brimfield Market USA

pages 76–77 white Carrara marble work surface, sink and spout, lacquered mdf cupboards and drawer units in Pawson House, London, all designed by John Pawson; pasta pan Divertimenti

pages 78–79 chair cover fabric similar at Universal Towel Company; white bowls from a selection at Wolfman Gold & Good Co., USA

page 80 *below left*: Provençal chairs Paris junk shop

page 81 table and chairs similar at After Noah; flower pots Clifton Nurseries; white china Gill Wing

pages 82–83 chair cover fabric Russell & Chapple; metal table The Conran Shop; curtain fabric Designers Guild; white plates Wedgwood; lilac paint Sanderson spectrum vinyl matt emulsion Fascination 2309M

pages 86–87 *left*: wicker parlour chairs Palecek; myrtle topiary Christian Tortu at Takashimaya; white table junk shop; *right*: laminated Saarinen table and Tulip chair Frank Lord

pages 88–89 *left and top right*: room and furniture in Pawson House, London, designed by John Pawson; *below right*: loft dining area by James Lynch

pages 90–91 blind fabric Colefax & Fowler; plastic tablecloth John Lewis; wool throw Anta; chandelier Robert Davies; wall paint Country Cream Dulux

pages 92–93 sofa fabric Sanderson; green cotton check cushion Laura Ashley; cushion in blue cotton The Conran Shop; cushions in blue check JAB; throw Anta

pages 94–95 fabric swatches: narrow and wide cotton stripes Habitat; cotton check The Conran Shop; *main picture*: floral cotton covers, striped cotton blinds, linen and cotton rug Ralph Lauren, USA; ticking cushion fabric Ralph Lauren, USA and antique samples; *right*: metal daybed Colette Aboudaram, France; antique ticking on cushion fabric Bryony Thomasson

page 96 *main picture*: chair and sofa cover, cotton rug and paint Ralph Lauren, USA; cushion cover fabric Designers Guild

page 97 *left*: paint Olive and Calke Green matt emulsion mixed together Farrow & Ball, candle holder and side cupboard After Noah; *right*: blue cotton sofa fabric The Conran Shop, Paris; terracotta cotton armchair fabric Ian Mankin; interior design by Susie Manby

pages 98–99 Butler's tray table Crate & Barrel, USA, painted in Sanderson Spectrum Satinwood 50-23; *main picture*: blinds in ckecked cotton Designers Guild; wing chair covered in Tulipan Marvic Textiles; cream paint Buttermilk Dulux; white table Brick Lane market; *right*: checked terracotta fabric on sofa Manuel Canovas; wooden chest and metal planter Tobias and The Angel

pages 100–101 cotton calico Wolfin Textiles

page 102 *top*: sofa Nick Plant; *left*: light Lieux, Paris; *right*: basket chair Alfies Antique Market; mirror from Cligoncourt Market, Paris

page 103 wall paint colour Nantucket, Benjamin Moore USA

pages 104–105 *main picture*: wool blankets Anta; cotton rugs Habitat; cupboard Ikea; checked cotton chair covers Ian Mankin ; chairs A Barn Full of Sofas and Chairs; chandelier Wilchester County; shades The Dining Room Shop

pages 106–109 cotton drill Z. Butt Textiles

pages 110–111 *left*: chair in antique ticking Bryony Thomasson; interior design Susie Manby; *centre*: sofa Ikea; *right*: filing cabinet B.S.Sales; trestle table McCord; filing boxes, frames Ikea; metal chair and cover in cotton check Habitat; Bunny chair Designers Guild; wastepaper basket The Conran Shop

page 112 *left*: curtain fabric The Conran Shop

page 113 linen curtain fabric from a selection Rosebrand Textiles, USA; myrtle tree Christian Tortu at Takashimaya, New York; sofa from a barn sale; wall paint Nantucket Benjamin Moore, USA

page 118 bed Portobello Road Market; chair Alfies Antique Market; white paint John Oliver

page 119 old linen Judy Greenwood

pages 120–21 cotton Laura Ashley

page 122 table Colette Aboudaram, France

page 123 striped cotton pillowcase Ralph Lauren, USA; patchwork quilt on bed Ruby Beets Antiques, USA; quilt on wall, Brimfield Market, USA

page 124 mosquito net Mombasa Net Canopies, USA

page 125 Tom Dixon light Gladys Mougin, Paris; Indian cotton bedspread Living Tradition, Paris

page 126 bolster pad John Lewis; cotton striped fabric Laura Ashley; wooden box Tobias and The Angel

page 127 bed Jim Howitt; antique quilt Judy Greenwood; pillowcases in cotton lawn Liberty; linen fabric on seat cushions Laura Ashley; white bedlinen John Lewis; paint Dulux Sandstone eggshell

page 128 muslin curtains Pottery Barn, USA; bedlinen Designers Guild; wool blanket Melin Tregwynt

page 129 bunkbeds Habitat Paris

page 132 *left*: shower curtain similar at Crate & Barrel, USA; *below right*: drawstring bag fabric Russell & Chapple; starfish Eaton Shell Shop

page 133 antique cupboard Colette Aboudaram, France; interior design Susie Manby

pages 134–35 bathroom cupoard Ikea; painted in Beryl Green 35-16 Sanderson Spectrum

page 136 wooden duckboard Habitat

page 137 *left*: peg rail Robert Davies; chair Alfies Antique Market; *top right*:shoe rack, pine mirror, butcher's hooks After Noah; brushes, soaps The Conran Shop; towels Muji; galvanized bucket The Conran Shop; medicine bottles junk shop; *bottom right*: linen basket Habitat

pages 138–39 cotton ticking Russell & Chapple; tea towels Divertimenti

page 140 jug from a selection at Sage Street Antiques, USA; peg rail Ikea

page 141 taps and bath Lassco; wooden bath rack Habitat; towels John Lewis

page 142 nail brush John Lewis

page 143 *top left*: tap and stone basin in Pawson House, London, designed byJohn Pawson; *top right*: outdoor brass taps from builders' merchants; *bottom*: taps and bath Lassco; bath rack Habitat

page 144 *left*: towels, flannels and robe Designers Guild; *right*: towels John Lewis

page 145 bathroom by James Lynch ; bath Lassco; shower taps Nicholls and Clarke; tins Alfies Antique Market

pages 146–47 cutlery Designers Guild; beaker Heal's; blanket Anta; table Brick Lane Market

page 149 tablecloth fabric Designers Guild; chair and table Clifton Nurseries

pages 150–51 cotton roller towel Universal Towel Company

page 153 beakers Heal's; tablecloth fabric and cushions Designers Guild

Suppliers

Architects and designers

James Lynch, D.A.D. Associates, 112-16 Old Street, London EC1

Susie Manby, 66b Elsham Road, London W14

John Pawson, 27–29 Whitfield, London W1

Bedlinen

The Chelsea Linen Co., P.O. Box 6, Tetbury, Gloucestershire GL8 8EJ
Fabulous linen sheets, and other white cotton bedlinen.

Cologne & Cotton, 791 Fulham Rd, London SW6 (mail order)
Beautiful bedlinen in plain white and colours; also towels and robes.

Damask, Broxholme House, New King's Rd, London SW6
Cotton bedlinen plus accessories.

Designers Guild, 267–271 & 277 King's Rd, London SW3
The best brightly coloured cotton bedlinen designs around.

Judy Greenwood Antiques, 657 Fulham Rd, London SW6
Antique patchwork quilts, old white damask bed covers and antique beds.

Habitat, 196 Tottenham Court Rd, London W1
Really good cotton sheets in variety of colours, plus throws and bedcovers.

Heal's, 196 Tottenham Court Rd, London W1
Really good quality beds, white cotton sheets, luxurious duvets and pillows.

Ikea, 2 Drury Way, North Circular Rd, London NW10
Good range of bedframes, including bunks and a stylish, simple four poster.

Ralph Lauren Home Collection, 4th Floor, Harvey Nichols, Knightsbridge, London SW1
Smart bedlinen and accessories.

The Monogrammed Linen Shop, 168 Walton St, London SW3
Pillows and sheets embroidered with your initials.

The Shaker Shop, 322 Kings Road, London SW3
Simple checked bedlinen, plus Shaker style beds.

Tobias and The Angel, 68 White Hart Lane, London SW13
Antique linen: old linen pillowcases, and sheets., plus antique wooden bedsteads.

Melin Tregwynt, Castle Morris, Haverfordwest, Pembrokeshire SA62 5UX
Checked wool blankets in wonderful blues, greens and yellows.

The White Company, Unit 19c, The Coda Centre, 189 Munster Rd, London SW6
White bedlinen, with sets in pure linen.

Fabric

Anta, Fearn, Tain, Ross-shire, Scotland
Boldly coloured tartans in wool and silk.

Laura Ashley, 256–258 Regent Street, London W1
Wide selection of coloured cotton in prints and weaves; also upholstery linen.

The Blue Door, 77 Church Rd, Barnes, London SW13 9HH
Blue-and-white Swedish checks, stripes and plains in cotton and linen.

Jane Churchill, 51 Sloane St, London SW1
Decorative cottons.

Colefax and Fowler, 39 Brook St, London W1
Traditional floral and checked cotton.

The Conran Shop, Michelin House, 81 Fulham Rd, London SW3
Brightly coloured Indian cottons plus wide range of other cotton textures.

Designers Guild, 267–271 & 277 Kings Rd, London SW3
Bright cottons, in florals and checks.

Pierre Frey, 251–53 Fulham Road, London SW3
Decorative fabrics in good colourways.

Habitat, 196 Tottenham Court Rd, London W1
Plain, checked and striped cottons.

R.Halstuk Textiles, 35 Brick Lane, London SE1
A wide range of dress fabrics plus lightweight denims.

JAB International, Chelsea Harbour Design Centre, London SW10
A wide range of textures and woven checked cottons.

Cath Kidston, 8 Clarendon Cross, London W11
Bright floral fifties-inspired cotton.

Liberty, Regent Street, London W1
Wide range of furnishing fabrics, plus floral printed cotton lawn.

McCulloch & Wallis, 25 Dering St, London W1
Distributors of Bennett Silks: a huge variety in creams and bright colours.

Manuel Canovas, 2 North Terrace, Brompton Rd, London SW3
Bold floral prints, and wonderful coloured weaves for upholstery.

Malabar Cotton Co., The Coach House, Bakery Place, 119 Altenburg Gardens, London SW11
Colourful Indian checks, stripes and plain cottons.

Marvic Textiles, Unit 1, Westpoint Trading Estate, Alliance Rd, Acton, London W3
Good weaves in wide range of colours for upholstery.

Old Town, 32 Elm Hill, Norwich NR3 1HG
Gingham checks by the metre.

Osborne & Little, 304–308 Kings Rd, London SW3
Cottons and good upholstery weaves.

Pukka Palace, 174 Tower Bridge Rd, London SE1
Checked, plain and striped cottons.

Sanderson, 112–120 Brompton Rd, London SW3
Striped and checked cottons for upholstery and curtains.

Muriel Short, Hewitts, Elmbridge Rd, Cranleigh, Surrey
Good selection of muslin and plain linens in bright colours.

Flooring

Crucial Trading, 77 Westbourne Park Rd, London W2
Floor coverings in coir, sisal, jute and other natural textures.

Fired Earth, 117–19 Fulham Rd, London SW3
Natural coir and sisal flooring plus all kinds of terracotta flooring.

Hardwood Flooring Co, 146–152 West End Lane, London NW6
Oak, ash, beech, maple, teak, mahogany, pitchpine.

Ikea, 2 Drury Way, North Circular Rd, London NW10
Mats and rugs in wool and cotton, plus laminate and wooden flooring.

Junkers, Unit 3–5, Wheaton Court Commercial Centre, Wheaton Rd, Witham
Tough, stylish wooden strip flooring.

Lassco, 101–106 Britannia Walk, Islington, London N1
Reclaimed timber, including old oak floorboards, plus stone and terracotta floor tiles.

Roger Oates, The Long Barn, Eastnor, Ledbury, Herefordshire HR8 1EL
Wool runners, plus mats and rugs.

Paris Ceramics, 583 Kings Rd, London SW6
Stone and terracotta flooring.

Sinclair Till, 791–793 Wandsworth Rd, London SW8
Natural floor coverings in coir and sisal, plus wooden and composite floors, and linoleum .

Walcot Reclamation, 108 Walcot Street, Bath BA1 5BG
Hardwood planking, strip, block and parquet flooring, also York stone flags.

Waveney Apple Growers, Aldeby, Beccles, Suffolk NR33 0BL
Handwoven rush flooring.

Food

Carluccio's, 8a Neal St, Covent Garden, London WC2
Wonderful Italian breads, pasta, cheese, oils and fresh wild mushrooms.

Steve Hatt, 8 Essex Rd, London N1
The best fresh fish and shellfish.

Neals Yard Dairy, 7 Shorts Gardens, London WC2
Excellent British cheeses.

Monmouth Coffee House, 27 Monmouth St, London WC2
Really good coffees.

Furniture/accessories

Action Handling, The Maltings Industrial Estate, Station Rd, Sawbridgeworth, Herts CM21 9JY
Metal mesh storage and office and factory furniture.

Ruth Aram, 65 Heath St, Hampstead, London NW3
Modern furniture and accessories.

Aero, 96 Westbourne Grove, London W2
Modern furniture, including Jacobsen-style chairs, china, glass and bright plastic accessories.

Aria, 133 Upper St, London N1
Contemporary furniture and accessories.

The Conran Shop, Michelin House, 81 Fulham Rd, London SW3
Ideas for seating, and dining; great baskets, bath towel, china and lots of outdoor living ideas, such as lanterns, flower pots, folding chairs.

Robert Davies, Restineas Farm, Garker, St Austell, Cornwall PL26 8YA
Made-to-order peg rails ad other decorative wooden accessories.

Designers Guild, 270–271 & 277 Kings Rd, London SW3
Modern upholstery, painted furniture plus brightly coloured cushions, stationery, tableware and baskets.

Eaton Shell Shop, 30 Neal St, London WC2

If you can't get to the beach come here for all sorts of shells and rocks.

Egg, 36 Kinnerton Street, London SW1
Simple accessories and fabrics with an ethnic feel.

Angela Flanders, Highfield House, Lower Blandford Road, Shaftesbury, Dorset, SP7 8NR (mail order)
Hand made pot pourri materials and essential oils .

Habitat, 196 Tottenham Court Rd, London W1.
All sorts of stylish furniture for the home, plus a good selection of frames and shadow boxes, also vases, boxes, baskets and bath towels.

The Holding Co., 243–245 King's Rd, London SW3
Storage ideas, including hanging canvas holders for shoes and clothes.

Jim Howitt, 42 Brushfield Street, London E1 6HE
Made to order wooden box beds.

Ikea, 2 Drury Way, North Circular Rd, London NW10
Everything for the home at great prices; lots of the furniture is flat-packed for convenience.

Cath Kidston, 8 Clarendon Cross, London W11
Fifties retro-style painted furniture, such as zinc-topped kitchen tables, dressers and and cupboards.

Next Interiors, 54 Kensington High Street, London W8 (branches throughout the country)
Good for china and glass accessories.

McCord Catalogue, Euroway Business Park, Swindon SN5 8SN
Great home basics, including simple trestle tables and kitchen chairs.

Muji, 26 Great Malborough Street, London W1
Simple furniture and Japanese-style flat-pack cardboard and metal storage boxes, stationery, bedding.

Nick Plant at Succession, 179 Westbourne Grove, London W11
Big comfortable sofas.

Purves & Purves, 80–81 & 83 Tottenham Court Road, W1
Contemporary furniture and accessories.

Paperchase, 213 Tottenham Court Rd, London W1
All kinds of paper sold by the sheet, plus other stationery ideas.

The Reject Shop, Tottenham Court Road, London W1
Good value furniture basics plus kitchenware.

V.V. Rouleaux, 10 Symons St, London SW3
Ribbons in all widths, textures and colours.

SCP, 135–139 Curtain Rd, London EC2
Contemporary furniture, including modern classic reproductions.

George Smith, 587–589 Kings Road, London SW6
Well-built, well-sprung upholstery, including really big comfortable sofas.

The Source, 5 West Quai Village, Western Esplanade, Southampton
Out-of-town shopping sheds with thousands of ideas for the home.

Viaduct, 1–10 Summer's St, London EC1
Contemporary furniture.

Sasha Waddell at Kingshill Design, Kitchener Works, Kitchener Rd, High Wycombe, Bucks HP11 2SJ
Swedish-style furniture with a modern edge.

Kitchen/dining

Ideas for equipment, china and glass:

BhS, 252–258 Oxford Street, London W1
The Conran Shop, Michelin House, 81 Fulham Rd, London SW3
The Dining Room Shop, 62 White Hart Lane, London SW13
Divertimenti, 45–47 Wigmore Street, London W1
Graham & Green, 4–7 & 10 Elgin Crescent, London W11
Habitat, 196 Tottenham Court Rd, London W1

Ikea, 2 Drury Way, North Circular Rd, London NW10
Jerry's Home Store, 163–167 Fulham Rd, London SW3
John Lewis, 278–306 Oxford Street, London W1
Liberty, 220 Regent St, London W1
David Mellor, 4 Sloane Sq, London SW1
The Pier, 200 Tottenham Court Rd, London W1
Peter Jones, Sloane Sq, London SW1
Summerill and Bishop, 100 Portland Rd, London W11
Gill Wing Cook Shop, 190 Upper Street, London N1
Woolworths, Head Office, 242 Marylebone Rd, London NW1

Kitchens and bathroom fittings

CP Hart, Newnham Terrace, Hercules Rd, London, SE1
Taps, sinks, baths of every shape and description.

Lassco, St Michael's Church, Mark Street, London EC2
Reclaimed baths, old sinks, old chrome taps and shower heads.

Aston Matthews, 141–147 Essex Rd, London, N1
A vast selection of taps, plus shower trays ,basins, sinks, baths, towel rails.

Nicholls and Clarke, 3 Shoreditch High Street, London E1
Taps, baths, kitchen sinks, etc.

Stovax, Falcon Road, Sowton Industrial Estate, Exeter, EX2 7LF
Distributors of Jotul.

Lighting

Aero, 96 Westbourne Grove, London W2
Modern lighting.

The Conran Shop, Michelin House, 81 Fulham Rd, London SW3
Wide range of contemporary lighting.

Robert Davies, Restineas Farm, Garker, St Austell, Cornwall PL26 8YA
American primitive-style painted metal chandeliers, made to order.

SUPPLIERS

The Dining Room Shop, 62 White
Hart Lane, London SW13
Checked candle shades and brass
candle carriers.

Habitat, 196 Tottenham Court Rd,
London W1
Wide range including desk lights,
hanging pendants, lamps and bases.

Ikea, 2 Dury Way, North Circular Rd,
London NW10
Large range of lighting, from lamps
and bases to pendant shapes.

Price's Candles, 110 York Rd,
London SW11
Huge selection of candles.

Purves & Purves, 80–81 & 83
Tottenham Court Rd, London W1
Contemporary shapes.

SKK, 34 Lexington St, London W1
Contemporary lights.

Wilchester County Lighting,
Staple Cottage, Vicarage Lane, Steeple
Ashton, Trowbridge, Wiltshire
American primitive style tin lights
and chandeliers.

Outside

Chelsea Gardener, 125 Sydney
Street, London SW3
Good for plants, pots and furniture.

Clifton Nurseries, 5a Clifton Villas,
Little Venice, London W9
Everything for a well-furnished
garden: clematis, honeysuckles, topiary
box, herbs, bedding plants; plus huge
range of flower pots and trellis.

Columbia Rd Flower Market,
London EC2 (Bethnal Green tube)
Held every Sunday morning: a great
source of cheap bulbs, cut flowers and
plants in season.

Langley Boxwood Nursery, Rake,
Nr Liss, Hampshire
Specialist in decorative box.

Provenance Plants, 1 Guessens
Walk, Welwyn Garden City,
Herts AL8 6QS
Plants by mail order including
foxgloves, lavender and auriculas.

*Florists guaranteed to have a good
range of seasonal and stylish cut
flowers and plants:*

Paula Pryke, 20 Penton St,
London N1
Wild at Heart, 222 Westbourne
Grove, London W11
The Flower Van, Michelin House,
81 Fulham Rd, London SW3
McQueens, 126 St John St,
London EC1

Paints

*Manufacturers with an interesting range
of colours:*

Farrow & Ball, Uddens Trading
Estate, Wimborne, Dorset BH21 7NL
National Trust colours, in a range of
period shades.

J.W. Bollom, 15 Theobalds Rd,
London WC1

Brats, 281 Kings Rd, London SW3
Mediterranean water-based emulsion
paint in vibrant colours with a
chalky texture.

Cole & Son (Wallpapers) Ltd,
144 Offord Rd, Islington London N1
Small range of period paint colours.

Dulux Advice Centre, ICI Paints,
Wexham Road, Slough, SL2 5DF

John Oliver, 33 Pembridge Rd,
London W11
Small range of excellent colours,
including bright Chinese yellow.

Sanderson, 112–120 Brompton Road,
London, SW3

Second hand
and markets

After Noah, 121 Upper Street,
London, N1
Factory and school-house furniture
and accessories, plus own-range spun
aluminum pendant lights.

Alfies Antique Market, 13–25
Church Street, London NW8
Everything from sixties furniture to
old fabrics, including second-hand
chairs, tables, china and glass.

A Barn Full of Sofas & Chairs,
Furnace Mill, Lamberhurst,
Kent TN3 8LH
Second-hand chairs and sofas.

D.A. Binder, 101 Holloway Rd,
London N7
Factory and old office furniture.

B.S Sales, 92 Old Street,
London EC1
Secondhand office furniture.

Castle Gibson, 106a Upper Street,
London N1
Factory tables, cupboards, and old
office and institutional furniture.

Decorative Living, 55 New King's
Rd, London SW6
Eclectic array of decorative antique
furniture and accessories; good for
things like old metal folding cricket
chairs.

Frank Lord, 78 Clerkenwell Rd,
London EC1
Junk furniture and accessories.

Bryony Thomasson, 19 Ackmar
Road, London SW6
Antique French ticking fabrics.

Tobias and The Angel, 68 White
Hart Lane, London, SW13
Decorative country furniture and
accessories, including metal watering
cans and other gardening equipment.

Markets that yield interesting finds:

Bermondsey, London SE1 (London
Bridge tube)
Held early Friday morning: antiques
plus junk furniture and accessories.
Brick Lane, London E1 (Liverpool
Street tube)
Held every Sunday morning: junk
chairs, tables, kitchenware.
Portobello Road, London W11
(Notting Hill Tube)
Held every Friday & Saturday:
sprawling array of stalls selling junk
furniture and accessories.

Foreign sources

Ruby Beets Antiques, Poxybogue
Road, Bridgehampton, Long Island,
New York, USA

Painted furniture, old white china and
kitchenware.

Brimfield Market, Massachusetts,
USA
Held the first week of May, July and
September; thousands of dealers and
great antique buys.

The Conran Shop, 117 Rue du Bac,
75007 Paris, France
Contemporary furniture like its
English counterpart.

Crate & Barrel, 650 Madison
Avenue, New York, NY 10022, USA
P.O. Box, 9059, Wheeling, Illinois
60090–9059, USA (mail order)
A wonderful source of good value
furniture and accessories, from simple
white clean china and glass to chairs
and beds.

English Country Antiques, Snake
Hollow Road, Bridghampton, Long
Island, NY 11932, USA
Period country furniture in pine, plus
decorative blue-and-white china.

Habitat, Wagram, 35 Avenue de
Wagram, 75017 Paris, France
Stylish furniture and home basics.

Colette Aboudaram, Manpenti,
83136 La Roquebrussane Var, France
Decorative country furniture and
antiques.

Hold Everything, P.O. Box 7807,
San Francisco, CA 94120, USA
(mail order)
Everything to do with storage from
linen baskets to canvas shoe holders.

Ikea, 101 Rue Pereire, F78105,
St. Germaine-en-les-Layes, France
For home basics at great prices,
including flatpack furniture and cheap
stylish kitchenware.

Lieux, Boulevard Henri 4, Paris,
France
Contemporary lighting, furniture and
accessories.

Mombasa Net Canopies, 2345
Fort Worth Street, Grand Prairie,
Texas 75050, USA
Mosquito nets to make romantic
bedhangings.

Benjamin Moore Paints, Montvale, New Jersey, New York, NY, USA
Good period style colors in muted shades.

Gladys Mougin, Rue de Lille, Paris 75007, France
Tom Dixon lighting and other work by contemporary designers.

Palecek, P.O. Box 225, Station A, Richmond, CA 94808, USA
Wicker painted furniture.

Pottery Barn, 2109 Broadway, New York NY 10023, USA
P.O. Box 7044, San Francisco, CA 94120-7044 (mail order)
Everything from furniture to decorating details, such as muslin curtains, china, cushions and candlesticks.

Rosebrand Textiles, 517 West 35th Street, New York, USA
Great value muslin, canvas, scrim and ticking.

Sage Street Antiques, Sag Harbour, Long Island, USA
Decorative period furniture and tableware.

Siècle, Rue du Bac 75005, Paris, France
Embroidered linens, cutlery and glass.

Takashimaya, 693 Fifth Avenue, New York, NY 10012, USA
Exquisite bedlinen, soaps and lotions.

Wolfman Gold & Good Co., 117 Mercer Street, New York, NY 10012, USA
Lots of stylish home accessories, including white china, crisp linen and silver cutlery.

Jane Cumberbatch's Best Value Top Twenty

Amy's Ardware, 48 Goodge St, London W1
A brilliant hardware store for basics such as metal buckets, brooms, pudding basins, wooden pegs, etc.

J.W. Bolloms, 15 Theobalds Rd, London WC1
Good paints and a huge variety of coloured felts.

Z. Butt Textiles, 248 Brick Lane, London E1
Denim, silk, calico, fabulous white cotton drill, muslin (all cheaper per metre if you buy at least 10 metres).

Habitat, 196 Tottenham Court Rd, London W1
Good cheap check fabric by the metre, kitchenware, cotton sheets and colourful bed throws; checked and striped cotton rugs.

Homebase, Beddington House, Wallington, Surrey FN6 OHB (branches around the country)
Flower pots, dustbins, kitchenware, storage boxes and other home basics.

Ikea, 2 Drury Way, North Circular Rd, London NW10
Basic wooden tables and chairs, white fold-up cricket chairs; also good value sofas, kitchen units, cupboards and work surfaces; cheap glass tumblers; boxed sets of plain white china; tough Swedish-style cotton checked fabric.

Peter Jones, Sloane Sq, London SW1
A mecca for fabric (everything from plastic tablecloths to muslin and cotton), bedding, kitchenware and endless practical essentials.

Lakeland Plastics, Alexandra Buildings, Windermere, Cumbria LA23 1BQ (mail order)
Incredible selection of kitchen accessories, from string bags to plastic containers.

John Lewis, 278-306 Oxford Street, London W11,
Part of the same chain as Peter Jones: brilliant kitchen and hardware department plus fabric, wool blankets, pillows, cushion pads, bolster pads, bath towels and sisal mats.

Limerick's, PO Box 20, Tanners Lane, Barkingside, Ilford, Essex IG6 1QQ (mail order only)
Everything from linen sheets to wool blankets and crisp cotton cloths.

McCulloch & Wallis, 25 Dering St, London W1R
Calico, muslin, gingham and a wide selection of haberdashery.

Ian Mankin, 109 Regent's Park Road, London NW1
Great for cotton checks and stripes, always has some on sale at great discounts.

Nottingham Office Equipment and Furniture, 217 City Road, London EC1
Great source of metal filing cabinets, coat rails, office chairs and tables.

Pongees, 28-30 Hoxton Square, London N1
Silk specialists: a wide variety of weights, plus beautiful coloured parachute silks.

Price's Candles, 110 York Rd, London SW11
A candle factory with just about every type of candle you could imagine; the creamy coloured ones are the best.

Russell & Chapple, 23 Monmouth St, London WC2H
Canvas, cotton, linen.

Staines Catering Equipment, 15-19 Brewer St, London W1
White catering china (mugs, plates, soup, bowls), giant colanders, saucepans and pasta pots.

Universal Towel Company, 1 Spa Industrial Park, Longfield Rd, Tunbridge Wells, Kent TN2 3EN
Smart blue-and-white roller towelling, sold by the roll.

Wolfin Textiles, 64 Great Titchfield St, London W1P
Cotton, ticking, calico, muslin and other utility textures.

Woolworths, Head Office, 242 Marylebone Rd, London NW1 (branches around the country)
Good for kitchenware and bright plastic picnic ware.

Acknowledgements

I want to say a huge thank you to **Jacqui Small, Anne Ryland, David Peters, Sian Parkhouse, Sophie Pearse, Penny Stock, Janet Cato** and everyone at **RPS**, who have worked like Trojans to produce *Pure Style*.

I am indebted to **Henry Bourne**, whose stunning photographs have captured the spirit of the book so perfectly.

I would also like to thank **Nick Pope** for the excellent cut-out photography.

Many, many thanks to my assistant **Fiona Craig-McFeely**, who has been an invaluable source of efficiency and support.

Thanks to **Tessa Brown** for making up the soft furnishing projects, and to **Jacqueline Pestell** for illustrating them.

I would like to thank the following people for allowing us to photograph their homes for inclusion in *Pure Style* : **Shiraz Maneksha; Ilse Crawford; James Lynch** and **Sian Tucker; John** and **Catherine Pawson, Pawson House, London; Marie Kalt; John** and **Claudia Brown; Peri Wolfman** and **Charles Gold, Wolfman Gold & Good Co.; Tricia Foley; Ellen O'Neill; Mary Emmerling; Gary Wright** and **Sheila Teague**.

My family have been unfailingly supportive, and have put up with many months of upheaval. Big hugs for my husband **Alastair**, my children **Tom, Georgia** and **Grace**, and my mother and father.

Index